# An Ethics of News

## A Reporter's Search for Truth

Also by the author

*Missions and Reconciliation* (1969)
*Faith at the Top* (1973)
*Memo for 1976: Some Political Options* (1974)
*The Spiritual Journey of Jimmy Carter* (1978)
*Land of Promise, Land of Strife* (1988)

Wesley Pippert, during a thirty-year career with United Press international, has covered three presidential campaigns, the White House, and congress and has served as principal Watergate reporter, chief Israel correspondent, and senior Middle East correspondent. He was granted two Harvard fellowships in 1987 at the Institute of Politics and at the Center for Press, Politics, and Public Policy. He was also awarded a National Endowment for the Humanities fellowship in journalism at the University of Michigan in 1975-6 and was a Congressional Fellow 1966-7. Pippert is a Phi Beta Kappa graduate of the University of Iowa and holds a masters degree from Wheaton College.

# An
# Ethics
# of
# News

## *A Reporter's Search for Truth*

Wesley G. Pippert

Georgetown University Press

Copyright © 1989 by Georgetown University Press
All Rights Reserved
Printed in the United States of America

Library of Congress Cataloging-in-Publication Data
Pippert, Wesley G., 1934–
    An ethics of news: a reporter's search for the truth/Wesley G.
Pippert.
    p.   cm.
    ISBN 0-87840-469-4. ISBN 0-87840-470-8 (pbk.)
    1. Journalistic ethics—United States. 2. Journalism—United
States—Objectivity. 3. Journalism—Political aspects—United
States. 4. Press and politics—United States. 5. Television
broadcasting of news—Social aspects—United States. I. Title.
PN4888.E8P57   1989
174'.9097—dc19                                                88-24700
                                                                     CIP

## Dedication

I was sitting in Tom Howard's study at his home in Beverly Farms on Boston's North Shore one afternoon, waiting for our wives. I pulled out a book, *Chronicles of Wasted Time*, by Malcolm Muggeridge. Its dedication read like this:

"Long ago I copied out from a Life of the French sculptor, Rodin, a letter he addressed to his wife, Rose, dated 24 August, 1913. It occurs to me now that in it he says to her exactly what I wish to say to my wife, Kitty, and that there could be no better place for saying it than here. So, transposing the names [as I am now doing anew]:

"'My dear Becky,

"'This letter is just to tell you that my mind is full of the greatness of God's gift to me when He put you at my side. Keep this thought of mine in your generous heart.

"'Your,

"'W.'"

# CONTENTS

# Introduction

Consider these situations:

—Early in the long 1988 presidential campaign, reporters from one newspaper staked out the townhouse where a candidate was believed to be spending the weekend with a woman not his wife, and a few days later, a reporter from a second newspaper asked the candidate point-blank whether he had ever committed adultery.

—In the same campaign, an anchorman and a presidential candidate engaged in a bitter exchange on live television.

Had the press overstepped its bounds? Was the press becoming too powerful?

Or, politics aside, how about these questions:

—Why isn't the decision-making process of huge corporations scrutinized as closely by the press as the decision-making process in political campaigns or even professional athletic contests?

—Why is it that the society pages of many metropolitan newspapers serving predominantly black cities are still filled with items mostly about whites?

—Why are many reporters very uneasy and even unfamiliar with basic concepts in covering the moral dimensions of public issues?

Do the media really get at the heart of what is going on in the world? Do we journalists unwittingly wear a lense that keeps us from a clear view of the world?

These questions are fundamental, and this book attempts to deal with some of them.

Most working reporters are not reflective. We are too busy with the breaking story or looking for a new angle on an ongoing story. But we ought to take a hard look at ourselves, what we are doing, what we are not doing, and why. What is our task and what are the implications?

In my view, the job of the journalist is to pursue truth. The journalist ought to understand the dynamics of truth—perhaps even before understanding the peculiarities of news. My colleague, Martin Linsky, a former journalist and politician who now teaches at Harvard's Kennedy School of Government, remarked to me, "Do you realize how controversial your point of view is? Many people, and most journalists, think reporters should merely observe and write their observations down. When you say the job of the journalist is to pursue truth, you are saying that reporters must put themselves into the story by making judgments about what is really going on."

This book is a personal document. For years, I approached my job with the traditional journalistic standards of accuracy, objectivity, and aggressiveness. But I felt I lacked a single transcendent principle to guide me in whatever my assignment, whatever story I was handling. Then it came to me: Truth, that's it. The job of the journalist is to pursue and publish truth. This discovery led me to study truth. What is truth? How can the reporter recognize it? What are the implications of seeking truth? Isn't it arrogant to assume that one has found even a measure of truth? What prevents the reporter from getting at truth? What is the power of truth, and thereby, the power of the press?

To leap ahead to my conclusion, I believe that the ethical reporter committed to truth inevitably will be drawn to issues dealing with justice and peace, no matter what his or her assignment happens to be.

Almost all of the stories and examples I use here are drawn from my own career, spanning four decades as a reporter. This is intentional. I knew the actors, the context, and the particular way in which I covered each story. The stories and case studies came from my assignments, ranging from two state capitals to three presidential campaigns to the White House to Congress to the Middle East. The ideas were honed during teaching stints as an occasional instructor at Virginia Tech and Gordon College, and finally, as a Fellow at the Institute of Politics and Center for Press, Politics, and Public Policy at Harvard, whose motto, after all, is "Veritas."

This book is divided into two parts: (1) a discussion of truth and its implications, and (2) the stories I covered, and the ethical problems I encountered.

The book is aimed, perhaps immodestly, at the working reporter, the academic journalist, as well as laymen. The working reporter may identify with much that I have written, and perhaps find even better examples than mine. I hope the academic journalist will find it of use in preparing a new generation of journalists. And perhaps it will persuade the average reader that the mass media are not totally ridden with cynicism.

I am grateful to John B. Breslin, S.J., my editor at Georgetown University Press, and Dr. Gordon Sabine, my mentor over the years and a journalist par excellence; to Kelly Clark, a philosopher, and Cliff Christians and Cynthia Ellenwood, journalism ethicists, who critiqued the manuscript. My thanks also to the following individuals who read various chapters: to Jody Powell, former White House press secretary (chapter 7); Frank Eleazer, former UPI House chief in Washington (chapter 8); James Dorsey, my colleague and a top foreign correspondent (chapter 9); and Regina Keeney, counsel to the Senate Communications subcommittee (part of chapter 5). I am grateful to all of my colleagues and students, for helping shape me and my ideas. I am especially grateful to David Aikman, Bob Andrews, Cal Thomas, Gerald Nadler, Patricia Behre, James Dorsey, and Russ Pulliam, as close friends as they are crack journalists.

Wes Pippert

Cambridge, Mass.
1987

CHAPTER 1

# Truth and Untruth

The job of the journalist is to pursue and publish truth: no more, and certainly no less. Whether a member of the mass media in Washington, or working for a rural weekly newspaper or a special interest publication, the journalist ought always to seek out and report the truth. The same goes for a political commentator, an investigative reporter, or a specialized journalist.

There is a question of purity here. The journalist does not deal in an ordinary product. The commodity is truth itself. In his farewell note to his staff at the *New Yorker* magazine on 12 February 1987, William Shawn said that "what matters most is that you and I, working together, have tried constantly to find and say what is true."

Knowing the nature of truth, in my view, is more important than knowing about news. More important than a nose for news is a hunger for truth. In this chapter, I attempt to set forth what truth is and what it is not, and what external and internal barriers hinder the journalist in pursuing truth. As British journalist Gerald Priestland says: "Although we may never arrive at the central core of the truth, we must never foreclose on it or assume that the little progress we can make towards it is not worthwhile."[1]

## NEWS AND TRUTH

All news ought to be true, but obviously, all truth is not news. News can be defined as (1) the significant, or (2) the sentimental—anything that affects or interests "the Kansas City milkman" (as old UP hands used to say) or the Washington decision-maker. News, whether the significant or the sentimental, also has the underlying element of (3) being timely.

Other factors come into play. Generally, journalists will agree on what hard news to cover—almost any journalist would cover the prime minister's speech to Parliament, a plane crash, an earthquake, the World Series. But a reporter's *selection* of what features or special reports or analyses to do often reflects that reporter's feelings more strongly than he or she may admit. There is also an accidental dimension to news. Whether a certain event becomes news on a certain day may depend simply on whether a reporter happened to be present.

It has been said that journalists write the first rough draft of history. Philip Gillon, a lawyer in South Africa who moved to Israel and became a columnist for the *Jerusalem Post,* perhaps said it best: "The news is a superficial view of the history of the preceding day. Newsmen cannot do as much research as historians in their studies; but, within limits allowed them by time, geography, censors and deadlines, they try to give the public a slice of history."[2]

One of the most frequent criticisms of the press that I encounter is that it prints only bad news. Even Pope John Paul II urged the media not to be obsessed with bad news but to give good news its fair play. "Give good news a chance," he said. "Make it at least as thrilling as bad news and search for whatever good may be hidden behind tragedy."[3] It is understandable why news often is bad. For the news is a tornado, an air crash, the death of a famous person. It may not be news that 999 of one thousand students showed up for class today, but it definitely would be news that one student was absent because he was found to be suffering from AIDS.

The news actually may not be as bad as people think it is. I once made an informal survey of the *Washington Star* for a week, rating stories as to whether they were good news, bad news, or neutral. The biggest category was the neutral, and the "good news" stories outnumbered the "bad news." Gerald Priestland has quantified it, estimating that news generally is about 40 percent bad, 30 percent good, and 30 percent neutral. "A good deal depends on your social and political philosophy," Priestland adds;[4] the ethical journalist, "for example, ought to be able to show that what is good and virtuous and true is as attractive and intelligible as what is evil, corrupt and false."[5]

## What Truth Is Not

### A Lie

A lie is not truth. And a lie told to get at the truth is still a lie. Moral philosopher Sissela Bok offers one of the best arguments against lying: "it is easy to tell a lie but hard to tell only one."[6] Mrs. Bok says that lying may be justified *only* when it can survive the very stringent test of justification by "reasonable persons."[7] These times are extremely rare, she says.

But what of those occasions when journalists lie or engage in deception to get information in order to expose wrong-doing or corruption? Clifford Christians deals with this pursuit of what he calls "tragic truth" in discussing two cases: the purchase of the Mirage Bar by two disguised *Chicago Sun-Times* reporters in order to learn about payoffs and kickbacks, and Janet Cooke's story about the fictitious boy drug addict in the *Washington Post.*[8]

Christians, like Bok, favors a fairly rigid adherence to truth. He suggests Aristotle's "redemptive motif," such as Bill Moyer's "CBS Reports" program that gave voice to powerless people who had fallen through the Reagan administration's safety net:

> Moyers gave no moralistic sermons. He sought only to make the faces of the poor as distinct, and their voices as clear, as audiences typically hear and see from agents of the political establishment. The result was discernment and proper purgation on the occasion of tragedy . . .
>
> Instead of deceptive practices to shake loose the story . . . I propose a normative framework of a radically different sort. On one level, grasping it involves a careful schooling in the logic of tragedy and an interpretive model anchored in discernment and redemptiveness. In the deepest sense, the only option is spiritual renewal. I call for a fundamental re-ordering of a professional culture, in an era when the notion of fundamental commitments is itself scarcely understood . . . one constructs a normative theory as an act of conscience, believing that such formalities will radicalise and renew the idea of truth-telling over the long term.[9]

## Mere Objectivity

"Objectivity" is often held up as a journalistic ideal. But emphasis on "objectivity" can obscure truth at times. Objectivity may become the mere presentation of two sides of an issue in a way that distorts the proportionate importance of each.

For example, a handful of strident demonstrators, representing only themselves, can be mentioned so high in the story as to exaggerate their importance. During the 1980 Carter campaign, much of which was conducted in the South, isolated groups of white-clad members of the Ku Klux Klan occasionally appeared in view of the presidential motorcade. We campaign reporters generally mentioned them, often prominently, in our stories. But the KKK did not represent the truth of that campaign.

On the other hand, the reporter must also be alert to the "lone voice crying in the wilderness" who may have a greater grasp of truth at the moment of *kairos,* or the critical moment. Henry Fonda played such a person in the movie, *Twelve Angry Men,* in which he was the lone juror who had initial doubts about the young man's guilt. The truth was not readily apparent to the other eleven jurors. Eventually, all twelve jurors voted for acquittal. Whistleblowers may have a clearer grasp of truth than bureaucratic superiors who would muzzle them.

Reporters must exercise a great deal of discernment in deciding what to cover and how to cover it. They must do far more than merely report two opposing viewpoints in the name of "objectivity" and conclude that they thereby have fulfilled their obligation.

## Mere Verbiage

A few well-chosen words often get closer to the heart of the story than a lot of verbiage. As Kenneth L. Pike, the University of Michigan and Wycliff Institute linguist, has said, truth is not be be confused with a mass of data or information.[10] Many students have discovered to their dismay that they could not cover their lack of knowledge in an essay examination merely by pouring out a torrent of often irrelevant words.

The Creation story in Genesis is told in about three hundred words. Francis T. Leary, the late managing editor of United Press International, used to hold up the example of David and Goliath (1 Sam. 17:31-49) as a model of concise reporting and writing. In about 350 words, the writer tells the story with staccato terseness. The last verse is especially graphic: "And David put his hand in his bag and took out a stone, and slung it, and struck the Philistine on his forehead; the stone sank into his forehead, and he fell on his face to the ground."

There is another reason to strive for terseness in relaying truth. With today's deluge of information that inundates people's attention, it is imperative that the modern journalist learn to state the truth quickly and concisely. There obviously is a need for the TV documentary, the one thousand-word wire dispatch and the ten thousand-word magazine article. But many journalists do not have that luxury. There are literally thousands of stories competing every day to make television's network news or the front page of the nation's newspapers. The story that is lean and to the point stands a better chance of doing so.

There is constant battle between reporters who insist that they need several hundred or thousand words for their story, and editors who insist with equal vigor that they do not. Many network reporters demonstrate that even a complicated issue can be encapsulated in three minutes or less. Because the nature of media varies, the amount of time or space that can be devoted to an issue also varies. Television must use a few words (probably three hundred or fewer) and dramatic film footage to tell a story. Daily newspaper stories can't exceed several hundred words and a dramatic still shot or two. Magazines may use thousands of words and take several weeks to prepare an article. I am convinced that each of the media, given their limitations, is capable of capturing and communicating at least a morsel of truth.

## Mere Accuracy

Truth is not to be confused with mere accuracy. Even accurate facts can mislead or deceive.

For example, in November 1981 the Reagan White House was unhappy with Arthur S. Flemming, chairman of the U.S. Civil Rights Commission, because of Flemming's outspoken and aggressive support of busing for desegregation purposes, of affirmative action programs and other civil rights issues. According to law, the chairman serves at the pleasure of the president. Flemming was a life-long Republican who had served in the Eisenhower cabinet. One morning, Flemming called me aside and told me a White House messenger had just delivered a message saying he was being replaced as chairman. I asked Flemming if that meant he had been fired. Of course, he said. I quickly called the UPI general desk and learned that the White House press office had just issued a release saying merely that Reagan would nominate Clarence Pendleton as the new chairman of the commission. There was no mention of Flemming and the controversy surrounding him.

I know from long experience how the White House press room operates; often the reporters depend solely on information the press secretary provides. If reporters had relied only on the White House statement, even though it was correct, they might have treated the matter as a routine personnel change and the public would have been misled. Such a story might have stated:

WASHINGTON—President Reagan will nominate Clarence Pendleton, a California black, as chairman of the U.S. Civil Rights Commission, the White House announced today. Pendleton will succeed Arthur Flemming.

This would have been accurate but hardly would have been the full truth. As it was, we dispatched a story saying:

WASHINGTON—President Reagan today fired Arthur Flemming as chairman of the U.S. Civil Rights Commission following long White House objection to Flemming's civil rights views.

That story was accurate—and true.

As I illustrate in chapter 9, the distinction between accuracy and truth is often blurred in the volatile Middle East. The Israelis tend to approach truth with a Western-like commitment to precision and accuracy. The Arabs, on the other hand, often exaggerate their statements, making their accounts highly suspect in foreign correspondents' minds. The Arabs employ hyperbole and rhetorical flourish, not necessarily to deceive but as a way to convey deep feeling. If they exaggerate the number of people killed in an attack or battle, perhaps others will feel as acutely as they do. It is a cultural matter. The eastern Mediterranean region is given to such hyperbole: One need only contrast the tales of Oriental mythology with the stark realism of the Hebrew Scriptures.

I am not condoning inaccuracy. I am simply attempting to point out the limitations of mere accuracy.

The *Washington Post* was condemned in 1981 after it was found that its reporter, Janet Cooke, had written a story about a fictitious eight-year-old boy named Jimmy whose mother's boy friend gave him shots of drugs. The furor over the fiction obscured the greater truth that the story was describing—that drugs are a serious problem among even young boys and girls. Cooke was forced to surrender her Pulitzer Prize.

"The plays of Edward Albee and Harold Pinter tell me more about the human condition than all the facts and statistics produced by social scientists. Yet these plays are not particularly realistic," writes Philip Morgan (personal letter, 10 Feb. 1980). In the 1960s and 1970s, there was a tendency among people ostensibly concerned about relationships to "be honest" and to "speak the truth in love." Often, such "honesty" resulted in the bludgeoning of other people's feelings. There is more to truth than just accuracy; there is its emotive content as well.

Jacques Ellul, the French political philosopher, condemning the modern practice of using facts as the criterion of truth, wrote: "People take the fact . . . then they divinize it, and it is suddenly imposed on a whole category of men, without difficulty, because modern people are ready to fall down and worship facts. Everyone takes it for granted that fact and truth are one."[11]

"Truth is very much more than the obvious facts," Priestland says.[12] He challenges journalists who find out and record the answers to the classic questions: who? what? when? where? and, if possible, how? and why? He says, "simply answering these four questions can be a great deal more difficult than you might imagine. The last two are often impenetrable, though they are the most important."[13]

## The Pseudo-event

Journalists often are besieged by "pseudo events" held simply to get publicity. These events sometimes bear little resemblance to truth. A special interest group, skilled in using the media, can call a press conference, have it announced in the day book of the city news wires, and get wide coverage—even though the event does not warrant it.

Senators often call news conferences while Congress is in recess in order to seek coverage of a hyped event that otherwise would be ignored. The White House "photo opportunities," in which reporters and photographers are allowed to be present for the first few moments of a meeting, can be misleading because they may give the impression that journalists were on hand throughout the entire session. The president's innocuous remarks during the brief time the reporters are in the Oval Office often give no clue as to the discussion itself or the decisions to be made. Or, the president, aware that reporters are listening during these photo sessions, will say something he wants them to hear and report. The reporter must attend these photo sessions if possible, for they add to the body of information he or she is assembling about the president; yet, the reporter must also be aware of their shortcomings.

Events of real significance often go uncovered because the participants are not sophisticated in the ways of attracting coverage or engage in tactics that prohibit coverage. On the other hand, President Carter complained on one occasion that an important trade bill received almost no attention or coverage in the mass media.

Ironically, because press spokesmen rarely give blatantly false information, they have great credibility. The most effective lobbyist these days is not necessarily the person who wines and dines, but the one who has the information. At the same time, however, such lobbyists rarely give information that would contradict their point of view. The reporter must weigh not only the information itself but also the source of that information.

Malcolm Muggeridge, the British journalist, accused the media of creating fantasy instead of reality. In his 1976 London Lectures in Contemporary Christianity, Muggeridge said:

> The prevailing impression I have come to have of the contemporary scene
> is of an ever-widening chasm between the fantasy in terms of which the
> media induce us to live, and the reality of our existence as made in the

image of God . . . The media have created, and belong to, a world of fantasy, the more dangerous because it purports to be, and is largely taken as being, the real world . . . But fantasy is the creation of images and ideas which are not truth, which have no relation to truth, and which cannot have a relation to truth.[14]

## Arrogance

Reporters must not be arrogant and cocksure about their stories or assumptions. There are good reasons why reporters are often seen as hard-boiled. The typical journalist encounters enough pretense, pseudo-piety, and blatant fraudulence—especially among politicians and the highly placed in our society—to become cynical and suspicious of every official and every idea. Cynicism may be the occupational disease of journalists, but they ought always to be skeptical: questioning, testing, reexamining their stories. A German journalist once remarked to me that the journalist ought not to be cynical, for this leads to death and decay, but should be skeptical, for that assures life and growth.

The reporter ought to follow the example of Joseph welcoming his brothers in Egypt; the writer of Genesis says succinctly (42:16) that he tested their words to see "whether there is truth in you." Priestland says that a journalist "ought to be an unreliable partisan, since he should always be searching his conscience for the faults of the side he may feel inclined to favor, and for the redeeming qualities of the one he is inclined to blame."[15]

# WHAT TRUTH IS

Despite the foregoing comments, generally truth *is* objective, truth *is* factual. But these are not the main characteristics of truth. We need to go further.

"What is truth?" Pilate asked Jesus, but he did not stay for an answer (John 18:38). The ancients frequently understood more about truth than we moderns do. The ancients knew, in ways we moderns do not grasp nearly so well, that truth is dynamic and energizing.

## Trustworthy

The Hebrew word for truth is אֱמֶת *emeth*. It implies certainty, dependability, faithfulness. You can count on truth. It matches reality. A news story ought to be trustworthy and reliable. This is certainly one gauge of whether the reporter has captured at least a measure of truth.

## Enlightening

The Greek word for truth is 'αλήθεια *alētheia*, which means an un-veiling. This adds a critical dimension to our understanding of truth. In short, truth enlightens. Literally, we know more about the truth of a darkened room after the light has been turned on.

## The Heart of the Matter

It is not my intention here to provide a precise philosophic defini-tion of truth.[16] Suffice it to say, for our purposes, that truth contains the core, the essence, the nub, the heart of the matter. When journalists suc-ceed to the best of their ability in uncovering and communicating this kernel, then they have accomplished their mission.

When Grant Dillman, the Washington manager and vice president of United Press International, assigned me to the Carter campaign in 1976, few people knew much about Jimmy Carter. Dillman's only in-struction was: "This man may become president of the United States. We must define him to the American people." Dillman did not tell me to be objective or to keep my opinions to myself, but rather, "define him." In other words, discover the truth about Jimmy Carter.

Clifford G. Christians, communications ethicist at the University of Illinois, has said: "Truth ought to be the defining characteristic of infor-mation, as justice should be of social institutions and troth of marriage" (personal letter, 12 March 1982).

## Simple and Clear

Truth is simple. We write for "the Kansas City milkman" in a way that is simple and clear. Peter Gomes, the Harvard chaplain and ethicist, has said, "Every true thing has a simplicity about it, a clarity, a directness that reflects not the absence of complication, but complication tran-scended, overcome, transformed."[17] "Further," the Stoic philosopher Seneca said, "language which aims at truth shall be plain and un-adorned; there is nothing true at all in the rhetoric that makes a popular appeal. Its object is to sway a crowd and carry thoughtless hearers with it by sheer dash: It baffles scrutiny and is gone."[18]

In the story of David and Goliath, as translated in the Authorized

Version, very few of the words, aside from the proper nouns, are of more than one syllable. In arguing for shorter, simpler, Anglo-Saxon words—as contrasted to the polysyllabic, Latin derivatives—someone has pointed out that most curse words (always easily understood!) are one-syllable Anglo-Saxon words.

## Tied to Justice and Peace

The ethical reporter who is committed to truth will be drawn to the dimensions of peace and justice in whatever story he or she is covering. James Gordon Bennett fell short when he wrote in the *New York Herald,* "I tell the honest truth in my paper, and I leave the consequences to God."[19] Robert Blair Kaiser, professor and chairman of journalism at the University of Nevada Reno, has said, "If our stories do not help them be better people, happier, more able to make sense out of the chaos that surrounds them, then we're just playing games. And we're certainly not ethical" (personal letter, 26 Feb. 1982).

Time and again, the Bible links truth with other traits or principles. From the beginning, the writer of Genesis tied together mercy and truth (Gen. 32:10). The prophet Isaiah linked mercy, truth, and justice (16:5). The prophet Zechariah combined truth with peace (8:16). It was as if each leg of this monument—truth, mercy, justice, peace—required each of the others. In one memorable verse (85:10), the psalmist wrote:

Mercy and truth will meet,
Justice and peace will kiss each other.

The prophets also tell us what happens in nations where truth is not pursued—by implication, in nations where there is not freedom of the press. "Justice is turned back, and righteousness stands afar off; for truth has fallen in the public squares, and uprightness cannot enter. Truth is lacking . . . " (Isa. 59:14-15).

## Emancipating

Truth emancipates. "You will know the truth and the truth will make you free," Jesus said (John 8:32). This passage, and others like it, speak of God as ultimate truth. But there is a sense in which all truth frees.

We understand this better in a personal way. I am more afraid of what I don't know than of what I do know. Truth has a way of dispelling and defusing the fear and suspicion we often attach to the unknown. For example, uncertainty about an unknown medical condition often is worse than knowing the specific diagnosis.

In recent history, when the media unleashed the truth, it resulted in the eradication of injustice and wrong. The coverage of the plight of the blacks in the 1960s helped arouse the dulled conscience of the American people and led to the passage of a body of law providing rights for all men and women, regardless of color. The television cameras trained on the bombing of Southeast Asia and the Senate Foreign Relations Committee's 1966 hearings on the Vietnam war were the first big steps toward extricating our nation from that ordeal. As I note in chapter 10, the 1973 Senate Watergate hearings, in which the people could hear and judge for themselves the accounts of the president's men, were, in my view, the primary reason for the unraveling of the cover-up.

If reporters are committed to truth, it spares them from wrestling with their biases or prejudices. The issue is not, for instance, am I pro-Palestinian? Am I a Zionist? Or, am I prolife? prochoice? Rather, the issue is: what is the heart of the matter in this story? what is the truth in this story?

## Responsible

Responsibility of the press was the subject of *Absence of Malice*, a now-classic 1981 movie about an eager reporter and a willing editor who allowed themselves to be used by an aggressive government prosecutor hounding an honest businessman named Gallagher. When the prosecutor leaked that the businessman was "under investigation," the reporter and the editor hyped the story to read that he was a "key suspect" in the disappearance of a union leader.

They were correct to say that the businessman was under investigation, but the greater truth was that the businessman was being set up by a frustrated prosecutor whose probe was getting nowhere. To give "the appearance of fairness," the newspaper's attorney advised the reporter and the editor to get reaction from the businessman (played by Paul Newman). Then, "absent malice," the attorney said, "we may say whatever we want about Gallagher and democracy is served." The acquiescent editor said, "Let the people decide what it means . . . the people have a right to know." The attorney replied, "If newspapers published nothing but truth, they wouldn't need attorneys and I'd be out of work." Later, the reporter, Sally Field, was being interviewed by another reporter about her relationship with the businessman. "Just say we were involved," she said. "That's true, isn't it?" the other reporter asked. "No, but it's accurate," she replied.

The responsibility of truth underlies the freedom of the press that many societies espouse. In *Night and Day*, the story of an emerging mythical African nation, British playwright Tom Stoppard contends that freedom of the press is freedom—but "freedom with responsibility." In other words, truth also must be weighed in the context of whether a particular story enhances the national interest and the concerns of the people.

There are few pat answers to the question of when truth should or should not be published. In general, if truth contributes to justice and peace, as I note in chapter 9 on terrorism, then go with the story. If the story does not contribute to justice and peace, a second look is in order. If a story is so positive as to be flattery, so be it; if the truth is so negative as to be condemnation, so be it. Journalists should be much tougher on the person in public life who has assumed wider responsibilities in society and has chosen to live "in a glass house." The journalist need not pull punches or shrink from exposing what needs to be exposed. Conversely, journalists should be much more lenient toward average people, often unwitting and inarticulate, who bear no responsibility for the action that has propelled them into the public eye. I remember my zeal as a young reporter, phoning the home of a young co-ed who had just been slain, to get her family's reaction. I would not be that insensitive again. Jimmy Carter's nephew, a troubled young man, was hurt terribly by excessive and unnecessary media coverage when he had nothing whatsoever to do with Carter's presidency. Unquestionably, the glare of the press only hurt him more.

Truth will prevail, many philosophers have said. If the press has power, it is largely the power of truth. It is imperative that journalists pursue truth, but they also must understand its dynamics.

# CHAPTER 2

# Barriers to Truth

There are barriers to truth that people encounter every day. Some are external, such as censorship and secretive public officials. Others are internal, and more insidious because they deal with reporters' mind sets and world views.

## EXTERNAL BARRIERS

### Institutional and/or Individual

Sometimes these barriers are people, men and women who do not want reporters to get at the truth. Clyde Donaldson, one of my first bureau chiefs, said that most politicians prefer to operate in a vacuum unless any publicity were to be favorable. I have found no reason to change my belief in his statement in the thirty years since then. Reporters deal every day with people who do not want the truth to come out, generally for selfish reasons.

Recall Sen. Sam Ervin's remark during the Watergate hearings that men prefer darkness when their deeds are evil. Reporters must be dogged in overcoming those who would deprive them of truth.

Knowlton Nash, chief correspondent for CBC TV News in Canada, observed the tactics used by public officials:

Prime ministers, presidents, all political leaders, view managing the media as a vital precondition to their domination of the legislature, the public, and the whole political process. It's the same manipulating story in business, labor, or any field where someone is trying to persuade the public that their ideas or products are the best. They try to sell their ideas or products in the most glowing terms, emphasizing good points, ignoring bad points, and all too often economizing on truth. But stripped of the glowing protective colouration of public relations, what governments, politicians, business, labor and social activists of all kinds want is to have the media reflect their own self-image . . . in itself, a not unnatural desire. They prefer a sympathetic and sometimes sycophantic media, not an assertively independent media.[1]

## Censorship and Privacy

In a way, censorship and privacy are similar. Both militate against public disclosure. Censorship is the attempt of *institutions and governments* to prevent publication of certain aspects of their policies and practices. Privacy is the right of *individuals* to keep certain aspects of their lives out of the public domain.

It is not within the scope of this book to probe the legal questions surrounding censorship and privacy as balanced by the First Amendment, the people's right to know, the Freedom of Information Act. Rather, I want to sketch the questions in broad strokes, keeping in mind how censorship and privacy may keep the reporter from the heart of the story.

Sen. Sam J. Ervin Jr., while presiding at the Senate Watergate hearings, eloquently described an ordinary person's right to privacy. He was responding to former White House domestic affairs advisor John Ehrlichman as to whether Daniel Ellsberg's 1971 leak of the Pentagon Papers on the origin of the Vietnam war justified a break-in at the office of Ellsberg's psychiatrist.

"One of the prophets described the mountain of the Lord as being a place where every man might dwell under his own vine and fig tree with none to make him afraid" (see Mic. 4:2, 4). Then Ervin quoted William Pitt the Elder: "The poorest man in his cottage may bid defiance to all the forces of the crown. It may be frail, its roof may shake, the wind may blow through it, the storm may enter, the rain may enter, but the King of England cannot enter. All his force dares not cross the threshold of the ruined tenements."[2]

In the 1971 case of the *New York Times* vs. U.S. and U.S. vs. the *Washington Post*, the Supreme Court overruled the Nixon administration and said that the newspapers could publish the so-called Pentagon Papers about the Defense Department's secret study of the Vietnam war. Justice Hugo Black wrote: "Both the history and language of the First Amendment support the view that the press must be left free to publish news, whatever the source, without censorship, injunction, or prior restraints."[3]

The federal government often succeeds at censorship, despite the absoluteness of the First Amendment. The Pentagon prohibited reporters from covering the 1983 invasion of Grenada, and President Reagan defended the censorship by saying it was done to "minimize casualties."

In 1988, the First Amendment Congress, of which journalists were probably in a majority, went on record as opposed to the Supreme Court's 1988 Hazelwood decision, which gave school boards and school administrators the right to censor student newpapers.[4] And the congress supported the Supreme Court's 1988 *Hustler v. Falwell* decision granting great freedom to express opinion in the form of parody, satire and caricature. (*Hustler* magazine had written a preposterous, tasteless tale about evangelist Jerry Falwell, and he sued.)

The First Amendment Congress formally declared that censorship "is contrary to the spirit of the First Amendment and undermines the functioning of an informed society." It said the public has a strong interest in opposing censorship for the following reasons:

1. Promotion of individual liberty, intellectual development and self-fulfillment through free expression and unfettered access to the ideas and opinions of others.

2. Promotion of social interest in the attainment of truth by testing competing ideas in a free marketplace.

3. Promotion of our collective interest in participating in the democratic process as a self-governing people.[5]

But I have said that persons in public office and certain occupations must sacrifice their privacy to the extent that the public trust is invested in their positions. In addition to public office, there are other professions that also invite scrutiny of the people filling them: clergy, teachers, therapists, all have occupations that proclaim trust and fidelity and seek to shape and change attitudes and behavior. I would not only want to know but would demand the right to know if my therapist sleeps with any of his patients (although I would not go on a fishing expedition and ask, "Have you committed adultery with any of your patients?"). The press was right to probe the sexual behavior of television evangelists Jim Bakker and Jimmy Swaggart. In fact, the press was not nearly aggressive enough in exposing and probing the extravagant life styles of TV evangelists, who ought to recall that the gospel they preach emphasizes mercy toward the poor and oppressed.

The sacrifice of privacy, as moral philosopher Sissela Bok has pointed out, is drawn rather tightly around the individual officeholders and perhaps ought not be extended to their children. "The children of those who have sought public attention, on the other hand, often have a stronger claim to be left in peace," she writes. [6]

Privacy is a precious right when exercised by the individual, but it can become censorship and an enemy of truth when exercised by big institutions and governments. Paradoxically, the privacy of the individual often runs counter to the right of that individual to know what is going on in his government.

Freedom House, a forty-seven year-old organization dedicated to free institutions, estimated that in 1988, only 1.92 billion people in the world had access to a free press and 1.21 billion had a partly free press. On the other hand, 1.89 billion people lived in countries where the press was not free.[7] Only 24 percent of the nations had freedom of both press and broadcast, and 20 percent had partial freedom for both media. Fifty-six percent did not have freedom of the press and airwaves. The judgments were made not solely on the basis of whether the press was state-owned, as in the case of the British Broadcasting Corporation, but on the basis of the content of the stories. BBC obviously has great freedom.

The worst nations, Freedom House's Leonard R. Sussman said, were those with highly centralized control—Marxist-leaning nations in Eastern Europe, right-wing nationalistic governments in the Third World, and Arab nations. In 1987, Malaysia, Panama, South Africa, Fiji and Bangladesh applied strong new press controls. The Soviet Union (despite some liberalization under glasnost), China and other Marxist countries, continued to own all of their mass media and to exercise control over foreign and domestic journalists. In 1987, Freedom House said, 25 journalists were killed, 10 were kidnapped or disappeared, 188 were arrested, 51 were expelled and 436 were harassed. In all cases except kidnappings, the figure was higher than in 1986.

I once asked South Dakota Gov. Ralph Herseth his position on open meetings. He replied: "I am decidedly in favor of having meetings of state boards, commissions and committees open to the public . . . (but) state law does not make it mandatory that all such meetings be open to the public in toto, undoubtedly because there are times when a certain amount of background discussion is in the public interests for timing purposes and to avoid interruption. What is important is that the final results of such deliberations be made available to the press and public."

But is that a sufficient safeguard? Isn't the process by which a decision is made sometimes nearly as important as the decision itself?

Don McNeil of CBS, who covered both Moscow and the Middle East, has noted censorship of a different sort. He found that his New York producers were much more inclined to use a story perceived as being critical of the Soviet Union than a story perceived as being critical of Israel. "We have a mind-set," McNeil said of him and his colleagues, "but the network has a mind-set, too."[8]

## "Disinformation"

President Nixon's administration sought a de facto censorship of stories about Watergate by contending that national security affairs were at stake. The Reagan administration attempted a reverse version of this in 1986 in what came to be labeled "disinformation." The former tried to withhold information; the latter falsified it. *The Wall Street Journal* reported on August 25 that Libya's leader Muammar Khadafy was planning new terrorist attacks. Two months later, it was revealed the story was false and had been planted by the White House, apparently in an attempt to weaken Khadafy. Reaction varied. A French official, reflecting a blasé European attitude, asked, "So what's new?"[9] "Frankly, I don't have any problem with a little psychological warfare against Khadafy," Secretary of State George Shultz said. "You people in the news business enjoy not allowing the United States to do anything in secret if you can help it." Shultz recalled Winston Churchill's World War II comment, "In time of war, the truth is so precious it must be attended by a bodyguard of lies."[10]

Others were outraged. Sen. Richard Lugar, R-Ind., then chairman of the Senate of Foreign Relations Committee, said: "I think Khadafy is a menace. I think terrorism is a menace. The American people want to see this connection exposed and then suppressed. But I think our greatest strength is still that we tell the truth as a government, and there's credibility in what we say."[11]

Benjamin C. Bradlee, executive editor of the *Washington Post*, said: "In moments of stress between government and the press, the government looks for ways to control the press, to eliminate or to minimize the press as an obstacle in the implementation of policy, or the solution of problems. In these moments, especially, the press must continue its mission of publishing information that it—and it alone—determines to be in the public interest, in a useful, timely and responsible manner—serving society, not government."[12]

## Leaks and Source Stories

Let us define terms at the outset. "On background" means that we may print the information and attribute it to whatever source is agreed upon—for example, "a senior Israeli official" or a "key White House staff member." "Deep background" means that we may print the information, but with no attribution, on our own authority and at our own risk. "Off the record" means the material is for the information of the reporter only and may not be printed under any circumstances.

Leaks and stories attributed to anonymous sources often are severely and self-righteously criticized. Editors proclaim that henceforth their reporters will walk out of any meeting that is "on background" or "off the record." Generally, within a couple of days, the newspaper is printing source stories again.

In my view, with certain exceptions such stories often serve the cause of truth. Leaks and source stories provide the public with information they might otherwise not receive. Leaks and source stories may actually enhance the democratic decision-making process.

A source story, for instance, may permit a government official to float an idea for the express purpose of getting public feedback without having committed the government in advance to that course of action. Presidents use this tactic frequently in conversations aboard *Air Force One*. Henry A. Kissinger used this device while he was secretary of state, particularly during his "shuttle diplomacy." Leaks permit whistle-blowers to reveal corruption and wrongdoing by superiors at less risk to the one making the revelation. "Off the record" information, even though it cannot be printed, can be helpful to reporter and official alike, if, for instance, it were to reveal a scheme for freeing hostages. The official who shares information "off the record" often finds the reporter much more cooperative.

This is not the case, however, when damaging information is leaked about a competitor. An attorney general in South Dakota once leaked damaging information of a highly partisan nature about a competitor. I was a young reporter—and I used it. But I learned quickly that if a charge is made against a competitor, the person making the charge should be prepared to stand up and be counted.

## Bigness

Bigness often gets in the way of the truth. I am not claiming here that bigness is bad per se, but rather that it is very difficult to get at the essence of the large and the complex. Institutions suffer from this malady.

In Washington, many officials are afraid of or prohibited from speaking to journalists except through official spokesmen. I have spoken with some sources by telephone only without ever meeting them. It is even difficult to make contact by telephone in Washington on first attempt. Invariably, the official is (a) on another line, (b) in conference, or (c) away from his/her desk. Often, by the time the official returns the call—this is more true at the White House than in Congress—the deadline has long passed.

## INTERNAL BARRIERS

But internal barriers to truth are far more insidious than external ones. These barriers involve journalists personally—our attitudes, mind sets, world views, passions, the way we interpret our jobs. The mind set of a journalist may blind him or her to elements of the truth, a blindness so total that the journalist is not even aware of it.

There is a corollary question: Should reporters have some background, preferably academic, in the subject they are covering? For instance, is it good that so many sports broadcasters are former professional athletes? Must a music critic be a musician? Would such reporters write too technically? Or, should reporters' presumed talent for being "quick studies" get them by on difficult and complex assignments?

In some areas, such as nuclear weaponry, economics and finance, law, health, and other stories typical of a complex age, it is difficult to understand what is happening without some formal training in these areas. On the other hand, reporters who are laymen in the area of their assignments often work much harder at clarity than their colleagues who may have a degree in economics, law or medicine. The story must be clear; it should also have depth and be accurate.

There is a corollary to the corollary, too. Many academic institutions take the position that it is more important for a journalism instructor to have an advanced degree than years of experience as a working newsman. I am glad that the journalism instructors who helped me most— Neil Puhl, at Mason City High School, and Gordon Sabine, who held positions of academic leadership at Michigan State, Oregon, and Iowa, were as much at home in a newsroom at they were standing before a group of students.

I am not convinced that any one course is always superior. Arrogance or a patronizing attitude by either side is inappropriate. I am convinced, however, that there ought to be more interaction between the academic and the working newsman. I seize every opportunity possible to get into the classroom, as a student or as an instructor. I have taught at various times at Virginia Tech, the C.S. Lewis Institute in Washington, the New College in Berkeley, and Gordon College. I am a firm believer in sabbaticals, which many professionals but few journalists take. My own sabbaticals have been varied: an archaeological excavation in what was then Jordan, a congressional fellowship, a National Endowment for the Humanities fellowship at the University of Michigan, and fellowships at Harvard's Institute of Politics and Center for Press, Politics, and Public Policy. The ideas expressed in this book were tested just as vigorously in these environments as they were on my assignments.

## Words

It is easy for even the most talented journalists to lapse into stereotypes and clichés that harm the pursuit of truth. The words that journalists use are important, perhaps as important as their stories, in the pursuit of justice and peace. Words often are used with unfortunate nuances that convey more meaning than their literal definition.

One of my first editors, Jack Hagerty, told me: "There is no substitute for 'said'." Almost always, a synonym—such as *declared, stated, asserted, commented, remarked*—colors the quotation. So synonyms should be used sparingly and carefully. Let the quotation speak for itself. Rarely is it necessary to modify this. My repeated use of *said* in this book illustrates my belief in Hagerty's words.

Should an editor "clean up" the grammar or syntax in a quotation? The answer varies. If an ordinary person is unwittingly or unwillingly thrust into public attention, and his or her bad English reflects poorly on the person, I see no reason not to fix the errors. But if the person is one in high office, such as the president or presidential candidate, the use of bad grammar or poor syntax or pauses or a halting manner of speech may give important clues as to how that person's mind works. Quote such persons exactly, warts and all. I generally edit out "well" and repetitions in most quotes. But in the case of President Reagan, I would retain "Well," which he uses to start so many of his sentences. It is a characteristic of Reagan, and it seemed to me that when readers read that "well," they can almost see him tilt his head and shake it a bit as he begins speaking. Dwight D. Eisenhower had fractured syntax; Jimmy Carter's news conference replies and his extemporaneous statements were always precise and correct.

In the 1950s and 1960s, journalists frequently referred to "Red China" in contrast to Nationalist China. An editor seeing my use of the term asked, "Why don't you say, 'Mainland China'? It's more descriptive geographically and it doesn't wave a red flag at the reader." The editor was right, of course.

While I was working in South Dakota, there were frequent cloud-seeding projects to try to bring more rain to the parched prairie country. To add some sparkle to my writing about the project, I referred to the cloud-seeding scientists as "rainmakers." Then someone pointed out that "rainmaker" has the connotation of a magician or a seer, an inference probably drawn from Bing Crosby's movie of that name about that time.

I recall sitting on the UPI night desk in Chicago and frequently getting calls from a man saying in a sturdy voice, "This is Romanoff at the *Tribune.*" He invariably asked in what context the president or someone had made the remark attributed to him in one of our dispatches—in a prepared speech? in ad lib remarks? in a news conference? or, as occurred frequently at the White House, a remark blurted out on the way to the helicopter? Romanoff's point was well taken. Every story should list the context in which the remark was made.

The use of words can also leave a certain impression. Priestland says it is irresponsible to use loosely terms like *massacre, horror, bloodbath, rape, mugging, disaster, crisis, inferno, torture,* and *terrorist.* "They need to be handled by journalists today with the greatest care," he says.[13]

Sometimes we can use the right words and grievously err. I did this during my Watergate coverage by writing one day:

WASHINGTON—Former White House Counsel John W. Dean III said today President Nixon knew about Watergate etc.

I should have written:

WASHINGTON—Former White House Counsel John W. Dean III said today he believed President Nixon knew about Watergate, etc.

There is a big difference in these two accounts. The first seems to accept Dean's words as fact; the other says it more precisely and more fairly.

As a rule of thumb, if the content of the lead sentence is unchallenged, the attribution should be put at the end. If there is an unproven charge in the lead sentence, the attribution should go at the beginning so as to point out unmistakably to the reader the person who is making the charge. Compare the following:

JERUSALEM—There was no Holocaust, a self-proclaimed Nazi said today.
JERUSALEM—A self-proclaimed Nazi said today there was no Holocaust.

## Bias or Overcompensation?

Do reporters wittingly or unwittingly inject their biases and values into a story?

There is something subtle, and significant, involved in this question. Most journalists have the same world view: they embrace "the system," and, in general, the superiority of Western civilization and its values. Most journalists have attended the same types of colleges and universities. They cover the same news beats in the same way: the school board, city council, chamber of commerce, state legislature, Congress, the White House. They talk to the same kinds of people, and especially, they talk to each other. Journalism leads to a large number of "media marriages" in Washington. And the result is what A.W. Tozer, a twentieth-century Evangelical mystic, has called "cookie-cutter conformity."

Is it any wonder that journalists' stories are so much alike? Most stories in the mass media are more noteworthy for their similarity of perspective than for their differences. In fact, this similarity is so deeply ingrained that when a reporter takes a drastically different point of view than others covering the same story, he or she may go into panic for fear of being too far out on a limb.

Instead of fearing a variety of angles on a story, however, journalists should welcome diversity. The Scriptures are a model in this regard. The four gospels contain essentially the same facts about Jesus, but are written from vastly different perspectives and to different audiences. The sum of these accounts is a multidimensional view of his life.

When common culture results in a common perspective, often truth is compromised. This is the most serious bias and prejudice that journalists bring to a story, and is all the more insidious because it is so seldom recognized and labeled. But seeing it for what it is can be the first step toward dealing with it. I have been talking thus far about something that often is covert or subconscious. There are more overt ways in which bias or prejudice may affect a story.

There is a tendency nowadays, particularly in the sort of story that appears in the *Washington Post*'s Style Section, or in sports accounts, for reporters to inject themselves very forcibly into the story. The product reads very self-consciously. There is a place for journalism in which the writer becomes part of the story, but it must be done deftly to be effective. The reporter who may unwittingly become part of the story—as a hostage in a hijacking, as a person caught in a tornado or earthquake, or perhaps as a George Plimpton play-acting a role—may write a story in which he or she plays a critical role. But it must be written carefully and tastefully, not egotistically.

Robert Blair Kaiser says that "each reporter has his own point of view and each reporter's account of a person or an event will vary, depending on his own background, insights, state of being at the time— and whether or not he's had a fight with his wife that morning" (personal letter, 26 Feb. 1982). This is a view held by many people: that reporters have a fixed set of biases and prejudices that they necessarily must impose upon the story they are covering.

Timothy Crouse, an astute observer of the 1972 presidential campaign (which was the first of three I covered), wrote *Boys on the Bus*, the classic treatment of that campaign. He offers another view:

> It is an unwritten law of current political journalism that conservative Republican presidential candidates usually receive gentler treatment from the press than do liberal Democrats. Since most reporters are moderate or liberal Democrats themselves, they try to offset their natural biases by going out of their way to be fair to conservatives. No candidate ever had a more considerate press corps than Barry Goldwater in 1964, and four years later the campaign press gave every possible break to Richard Nixon. Reporters sense a social barrier between themselves and most conservative candidates; their relations are formal and meticulously polite. But reporters tend to loosen up around liberal candidates and campaign staffs; since they share the same ideology, they can joke with the staffers, even needle them, without being branded the "enemy." If a reporter has been trained in the traditional, "objective" school of journalism, this ideological and social closeness to the candidate and staff makes him feel guilty; he begins to compensate; the more he likes and agrees with the candidate *personally*, the harder he judges him *professionally*. Like a coach sizing up to his own son in spring tryouts, the reporter becomes doubly severe.[14]

Priestland says: "If the choice of facts is a subjective act, then inevitably there is no such thing as objectivity. But if a journalist is consciously striving to be fair, to avoid making a selection according to some loyalty outside the case in hand, then I do not think he can be accused of partisan bias, which is, I believe, a crime against the truth."[15]

Linda S. Lichter, researcher at Columbia University, S. Robert Lichter, political scientist at George Washington University, and Stanley Rothman, professor of government at Smith College, have conducted exhaustive studies of reporters' attitudes. They have studied professional reporters and editors as well as journalism students. Their 1980 study covered leading reporters and editors at the *New York Times, Washington Post, Wall Street Journal, Time, Newsweek, U.S. News & World Report*, television networks, and PBS. Forty-five percent of the respondents rated their family income while growing up as "above average";

more than 80 percent of working journalists seldom or never attend church services and only 8 percent say they attend regularly; 47 percent believe adultery is wrong; 54 percent describe themselves as liberals; 70 percent believe the private enterprise system is fair; 49 percent believe the structure of American society causes alienation: and 56 percent believe the United States exploits Third World countries. Said the Lichters and Rothman: "We found that leading journalists line up on the side of minorities, consumer groups and intellectuals and against both business corporate chieftains and middle America" (personal correspondence, 28 Jan. 1983).

All this presents us with a curious mixture of dilemma and paradox. The Lichters and Rothman imply that journalists' attitudes affect their reporting; Tim Crouse, as I have noted, suggests that journalists bend over backwards to be fair and often go so far that they are tougher on positions and officials they support than on those they do not.

My own feeling is that most journalists in the mass media try to cover a story as fairly as they can, but that their biases and prejudices are more at work in their *selecting* the stories and features they will cover. It is reasonable for us to conclude that journalists' attitudes and perceptions shape what reporters cover and how they cover it, even if in only minimal ways. What is required, at the very least, is an acute sensitivity that makes us aware of the elements of justice and morality present in a story. I am not talking about a journalist imposing his or her beliefs and values on the reader or listener. What I am contending is that to the extent that the reporter's values and beliefs shape a story, we ought to be aware of and probe them.

I believe the importance of *selection* is so critical that I discuss it more fully in chapter 5, on the power of the press.

## The Behavior of the Reporter

The study of the behavior of the journalist is—and should be—the shortest study of all. There is little to say. The journalist ought to be personally and professionally moral.

We obtain information in moral ways. If we are confronted with the moral dilemma of perhaps having to obtain information illegally, then we must subject that situation to rigorous ethical examination to see truly what is the more ethical course. Bernstein and Woodward faced this when they tried to elicit information about the Watergate grand jury proceedings, since such proceedings are always secret.

We treat agreements as if they were as sacred as covenants— whether with a source or with an editor or publisher. If a source tells us something off the record, we should not use that information. If a source tells us something and says he or she does not wish to be quoted, we do not quote that person.

Professional writers often take the same piece of information and "recycle" it into several stories. This can present ethical problems. When I returned from the Middle East, I wrote a book on modern Israel's fortieth anniversary. In order to promote it, the publisher contacted several magazines. One magazine chose to use excerpts from the book. Two other magazines asked me to write a special article for them. The general theme of both articles was to be "Israel at forty," although each magazine made certain other specific requests. I agreed to the requests of both, but did not inform either that I was writing for the other. As it turned out, both had "Israel at 40" emblazoned on their covers, with my pieces being their lead articles. Almost immediately, one editor was on the phone to me. Without giving the situation much thought, I had made the articles substantially different but had repeated three or four points in both pieces that I felt strongly about. Did I have a legal obligation to inform the magazines in advance that I was writing for both? Probably not. Did I have a moral obligation, since I knew both reached similar audiences? This is a difficult question, for it raises the problem of whether I had a right to tell one magazine what another magazine was planning. But on balance, I probably should have advised each magazine in broad terms that I was also doing "something for another publication."

(This also raises the question of whether professional speakers skirt ethical principles by using the same speech for convention after convention, each group paying the speaker for it.)

## Truth Will Out

Despite our noble intentions to pursue truth, we often run into blocks. These blocks may be institutional or governmental in nature, or they may be personal. But perhaps we need to look hardest at ourselves, our most basic attitudes and our manner of expression, to see whether we might be the biggest barriers of all in our pursuit of truth.

The reading public must recognize that, given individual frailties and institutional flaws, a single story is unlikely to present the whole truth. The reading public ought to compare and contrast publications and stories about the same issue. After speaking on nearly one hundred college campuses and to innumerable other groups, I find that a question frequently asked me is: "What publication should I read to get the truth?" It is unrealistic to expect the average person to read two daily newspapers, two weekly news magazines, and several opinion journals, as well as to watch television news. But ordinary people can go a long way toward getting at the truth by not limiting themselves to one story or, especially, one point of view. Even the person who reads only two publications with any regularity is likely to find truth emerging when the two publications are in agreement—or, paradoxically, in the collision of their stories. If one tends to be firmly committed to one point of view, it is imperative for that person to read the *opposite* point of view.

The reporter must recognize, as a practical matter, that rarely can he or she deliver ultimate truth or even most of the truth in only one story. Rather, the reporter builds a mosaic, with each story contributing to the larger truth. He will discover, with the English proverb and John Dean, that "truth will out."[16]

# CHAPTER 3

# Context and Perspective

The mass media often do not adequately put events into context historically, socially, economically. Often we do not write in depth, or more importantly, we do not write with perspective. The "softball" coverage of the Carter campaign illustrated this. So did the politically oriented coverage of the Watergate scandal. To the extent that media fail in this, the truth is sacrificed and the public is not served.

Journalists, especially newspaper and broadcast journalists, are handicapped by the demands of frequent deadlines. So we report whatever is the most immediate development. We often rely on only one source and write superficially. We pay more attention to controversy than context. Perhaps most serious of all, we often miss what is truly important because we are bound to traditional methods of reporting. We tend to look at people and events through political, institutional, Western, white, middle-class lenses; we seem less comfortable and competent in dealing with people and events that fall outside that grid. Because most members of the media have similar backgrounds and work for communications agencies with a similar outlook, we succumb to "pack journalism." Journalists are still prone to be the traditional chroniclers of record, reporting the police blotter and acting as unofficial "peeping Toms" on public figures. All these things get in the way of writing with perspective and in context.

Gerald Priestland has expressed concern about "the persistent superficiality" of journalism. The mass media's principal errors are, he says, "oversimplification, incestuousness, technical over-smartness and a lack of contact with their public."[1] Even in covering disasters, he says, "our concern about them tends to be restless, volatile, leaping from one end of the world to the other, arriving always too late and leaving usually too soon."[2] Priestland believes that the main function of the journalist is to build bridges—"across which people may reach out and understand one another"—and that journalists are far too busy doing this on an ad hoc day-to-day basis "to plan and execute any grand design of influencing the course of history."[3] "Most journalists have their noses down to the events of the day; they have little time to look ahead and see what is coming," he says.[4]

In some ways, the underground press, as distasteful as it often is, has come closer to reporting what is happening to the heart and soul of America than the mass media.

As I note in chapter 10, the press has not adequately reported the vast social and economic revolution that formed the backdrop for the various scandals (Milk fund, ITT) which were lumped together under the heading Watergate. I recall very few, if any, front-page stories in my hometown paper about the closing of the small country schools or the dairies or the stores on Federal Avenue. Such stories may have seemed inconsequential at the time, even to the people of Cerro Gordo County, but they were a microcosm of the great changes that were taking place in America as it grew from a rural to an urban nation.

The realization of the media's failure to report change adequately came to me with fresh force when I sought to share thoughts about Watergate and milking cows and candling eggs in a talk at Wilson High School, one of the most racially integrated schools in the District of Columbia, with forty to fifty nationalities represented in the student body. I felt woefully inadequate in trying to describe the America I knew as a boy. The day of the Sweet Clover Dairy and the family-size farm is about over in this country. So is the era of the one-room country school I attended for eight years—more than twice as long as any other institution I attended—and the mom 'n' pop stores like Sam Raizes'. There also have been drastic changes in life style in America: changes in behavior inside and outside the home and classroom, in sexual mores, in the use of drugs, in the rise of the occult. The mass media have not competently reported this revolution.

The yellowed newspapers we find in the trunks in our garages often reveal how little effect the stories that warranted front-page attention on a particular day proved to have. Hanging over my desk is the front page of the *New York Times* for May 14, 1934, the morning after my birthday. There were eleven stories above the fold. Only a few of them had long-range significance: the serious turn on the debt-transfer talks in Berlin, President Roosevelt's message to Congress about federal relief legislation. The Mother's Day celebration was an altogether fitting story for page one. But other stories dealt with a private mail plane setting a coast-to-coast record, Tammany Hall candidates, a kidnapping in Los

Angeles, a stock exchange regulation bill. These had little lasting significance.

Charles W. Walk, editor of the *Bismarck* (N.D.) *Tribune* and former editor of the *Kansas City* (Kan.) *Kansan*, points out the difficulty that journalists face: "How could we have known that the closing of a country school, or a series of country schools, was educationally or socially significant—at that time? How could we have known that the closing of all the local dairies over a 20-30 year period was economically significant—at that time?" (personal correspondence, 14 Jan. 1983). Paulette Pippert Cott, a news broadcaster in Sioux Falls, South Dakota, and formerly in Topeka, Kansas, observes: "It often takes years for us to see whether historical, social, and economic values will have any effects on our society."

But journalists ought to be more acute observers; they ought to take a moment to step back and ask: What is really happening here? What does it mean? The mass media ought not forfeit the function of perspective and context to scholarly journals and history books.

Let us examine some of the reasons why we fail to put stories into context.

## Overemphasis on the Political and Institutional

Many journalists, particularly in Washington, in state capitals and county seats, focus too much on political developments. It is to be expected that reporters cover officials who hold authority and make decisions; but in the process of concentrating on politics too heavily, we miss other currents. All government agencies and members of Congress have publicity personnel and offices to ease the reporter's job by providing information. But in depending too much on these official sources we often miss other, equally important developments and points of view. Not from one source but from many, through various perspectives and lenses, journalists can build a multidimensional mosaic that sets out the truth of the story.

Washington and other news centers are overpopulated with official press secretaries and public relations firms. In 1988, the Public Relations Society of America had 676 members and affiliates in its National Capital Chapter. Often they are excellent sources and a rich and reliable reservoir of information for the reporter. But all too frequently they are used as the only source for a particular story.

Government officials and special interest groups are skilled in issuing press releases that put their views in the best possible light. In almost three years of covering Congress, I accumulated five boxes of "handouts" from my assignment beat. The reporter seeking the truth must go beyond the handout.

In 1981, President Reagan's first major act was to propose a series of big budget cuts in social programs. When the Senate approved the cuts, one news agency wrote it strictly as a political story:

> WASHINGTON—The Senate handed President Reagan his first big political victory tonight by approving $40 billion in budget cuts that he had demanded.

But another news agency sought to put the cuts into historical perspective:

> WASHINGTON—The Senate approved President Reagan's demand for $40 billion in budget cuts tonight in what would be the biggest reversal of domestic social policy since the New Deal.

The wire services traditionally have been the pathfinders in setting the news agenda for the mass media. The networks and the daily papers throughout the country have followed their lead. In 1969-71, I was the UPI Washington overnight editor with responsibility for planning and editing the Washington news file for afternoon newspapers. In this capacity, I selected a half-dozen to a dozen stories to be included in our "editor's schedule," or "ed sked," a memo on the wire listing stories we particularly wished to call to the attention of editors throughout the nation. A rough breakdown of these stories shows that probably 75 percent of those on the "ed sked" were suggested by the reporter in the field, 10 percent by what other media were using, and 10 percent reflected my own ideas.

I sought regularly to include in the editor's schedule those legitimate and newsworthy Washington stories that related to people and the quality of life. Often the source of these stories was outside the government. But the newspaper wire editors frequently did not use the stories and preferred to use the more traditional political stories, many of which, upon examination a decade or more later, proved to have had little lasting impact. A complete survey of the "ed sked" news file for that eighteen-month period revealed a constant pattern of preference for stories with a political angle over those that dealt with people's everyday existence. Here are some examples (both wire services "log" about twenty to thirty major newspapers throughout the nation daily to see how their stories fared).

March 4, 1969—Eighteen logged papers used a story on the last illness of Dwight D. Eisenhower, and fourteen ran a story about President Richard Nixon's plan to reorganize the Cabinet. But none used a story on a study of attitudes indicating that Americans were willing to spend money for the poor, perhaps even at the risk of higher taxes.

April 22, 1969—President Nixon sent his first crime package to Congress, and twenty-three newspapers played the story. Only six used an analysis story reporting that unemployment was dropping much faster in slums than elsewhere and speculating on the reasons.

May 7, 1969—Ten newspapers carried a story that most members of Congress earn some form of outside income, but none of the logged papers carried one saying Agriculture Department data indicated that violations in the food stamp program were few.

May 20, 1969—The top story of the day logged sixteen newspapers, but testimony by a Columbia University professor that credit and preemployment information bureaus can, and do, destroy a person's reputation by spreading malicious gossip and faulty information got only two logs.

July 20, 1969—A story on taxes got sixteen logs, but American Bar Association testimony that "politicization of youth crime" would be dangerous and distressing was used by only three newspapers.

Aug. 29, 1969—An assassination story got fifteen logs, while a dispatch that President Nixon's nutrition adviser said poor families receiving help under the administration's proposed welfare reform would continue to be eligible for food stamps, received only seven.

Oct. 3. 1969—A railroad story got twenty-one logs, a dispatch on a scandal in military service clubs picked up sixteen, but Senate approval of the most sweeping coal health and safety legislation ever passed had only six.

Nov. 12, 1969—Stories on the forthcoming massive November 15 antiwar demonstration got fifteen logs; on the ill-fated Haynsworth Supreme Court nomination, ten; but a story on an American Indian task force, only six.

Nov. 13, 1969—As the antiwar demonstration approached, coverage of it got thirty-two logs; a story that a Great Society plan for fighting poverty was being given muted fanfare at the White House got only eight.

Nov. 25, 1969—The Senate vote on allowing the income tax surcharge to die at the end of the year was used by twenty-two newspapers; but neither a story on the leading congressional critic of the War on Poverty saying state and local elected officials must have greater control over it, nor a story on a welfare rights spokesman telling county officials, "We've got rights and we are going to use them," got a single log.

Dec. 5, 1969—Sixteen newspapers used a story on the My Lai massacre in Vietnam; only eight used a story on a Senate subcommittee warning that unsolicited credit cards are threatening to "produce a nation of credit drunks."

Jan. 21, 1970—Stories on a threatened Nixon veto of an appropriations bill got fifteen logs, and one on Nixon's consumer affairs adviser asking for a strong rule prohibiting supermarkets from falsely advertising "specials" received only five.

Feb. 12, 1970—The Senate Judiciary Committee meeting on the fate of the Carswell Supreme Court nomination got eight logs; a scientist's forecast on the one hundredth anniversary of the Weather Bureau that the next century would see "environmental management," none.

May 13, 1970—A story on new Justice Harry Blackmun speculating that he could swing the balance on the Supreme Court logged eleven papers, but a piece on a Ralph Nader student task force charging that ineffective laws let deceitful industrial giants pollute the air logged only four.

May 29, 1970—A story that the Nixon administration would not propose additional taxes picked up eight logs; a story on the Equal Employment Opportunity Commission's study of Spanish-surnamed Americans revealing a "caste system," received only two.

We must educate and sensitize not only reporters but wire editors and TV news producers to stories that go beyond the political and bring breadth and perspective.

In remarks to the 1977 White House correspondents' dinner (30 April 1977), President Jimmy Carter stated clearly the proper relationship of the government and the press to each other and to the people: "There is a great responsibility that we share, to understand one another as best we can, to tell the American people the truth as best we can, to realize the tremendous joint responsibility we have and the eagerness among the people of our nation to know about their own government—how decisions are made, the options we have, the successes and the failures, the hopes and the dreams, the deep concerns—and to reveal the prejudices that still remain is a major responsibility."

## Overemphasis on White, Western, Middle-class Culture

We have observed that most members of the mass media have similar backgrounds and perspectives. Most are white. Most have gone to the same kinds of schools. Most cover the same kinds of stories in the same kinds of ways.

This is also the great burden that many foreign correspondents carry, as discussed in chapter 9. Unfortunately, the real story at home in the States also is often "foreign" to the reporter. We tend to cover the

Chamber of Commerce instead of the person who really is the "big wheel," the one who turns the machinery behind the scenes. We tend to pay more attention to denominational statements purporting to speak for the entire constituency instead of observing the results of faith in action in individual lives and small groups. We report more from the Agriculture Department and county agents than we do about changing life on the farm.

At a 1983 conference on public policy and communication at the Ford Presidential Library at the University of Michigan, former President Jimmy Carter noted that top leaders do not always hear the public's sentiments. Carter said:

> One thing about being president or governor or a member of Congress is that the voices you here in a state capital or Washington are the strident voices, the narrowly focused, and the selfish voices . . . When you take a group of peanut farmers and organize them into a group and collect dues and send a representative toWashington to speak for them, that representative will speak much more narrowly than the farmers themselves because that is what he is supposed to do. But quite often, public officials only hear the voices of organized groups like these, and those groups speak much more stridently than the people they represent, the doctors or the lawyers or the peanut farmers.[5]

When I was a junior in high school, I was on the staff of the *Cub-Gazette*, the high school paper, which consisted of a page in the *Mason City Globe–Gazette* each Saturday, forcing us to reach for professional standards. It won an All-American rating that year. Neil Puhl, the adviser, encouraged us to run a weekly column entitled "Report to the Taxpayers," made up of items from our school classes. It was much more meaningful—and significant—to parents and students alike than a story on the school board's contract lettings.

## The Perspective of People

Ida McNeill was one of the most unusual broadcasters who ever lived. For many years, she ran radio station KGFX out of her living room in Pierre, South Dakota. Mrs. McNeill did not fit the stereotype of a prairie woman. She was urbane, well coiffed, and cultured. But she had a feel for the people who were her audience. If a rancher called to say a neighbor's cattle were in the wrong pasture, she would broadcast it. She called St. Mary's Hospital each day to see who had been admitted, why, and how the patients were getting along—a practice later adopted by the *Pierre Capital Journal* and other newspapers in South Dakota.

Nancy Boerman, a Californian who became a reporter for the *Williston* (N.D.) *Daily Herald*, describes her experience on the staff of John Andrist, editor and publisher of the *Divide County Journal* in Crosby, North Dakota, population fifteen hundred:

As a businessman keenly interested in the prosperity of his hometown, John has covered almost every store opening or closing, kept tabs on each season's wheat, sunflower and small grains harvest and the expansion or decline of any grain elevators in the county, followed city council and district school board meetings enthusiastically, and covered high school sports as thoroughly as if each school were fielding a professional team.

J.C. Penney and an appliance store closed, but three other Main Street stores in the three-block-long business district expanded during my stay in Crosby. Each change was recorded on the front page of the *Journal*, usually with photos of the owner or management and the new storefront or facilities. When the local Assembly of God built an addition on the front door of their church, John got it on film. When an old lumber business moved and the historic building was demolished, he recorded the structure's demise on a special photo feature page. When a historic Main Street building was threatened by construction plans for Crosby's second bank, John appealed to the community to save it—without success—by using the newspaper. When proprietors of the local theater could no longer rally enough help to dig it out of the red, the *Journal* covered each step in its change of hands to four local businessmen.

Weekly feature stories spotlighted local people, their work, their hobbies, along with changes like the coming of mechanical irrigation systems and Bill Bade and his honey bee business. Annual events were never taken lightly but always received prominent coverage—the Divide County Threshing Bee in August, the Divide County Fair in July, the Crosby Appreciation Day barbecue sponsored by local businessmen each fall (right out on Main Street—two blocks were closed to traffic) to thank their customers for their patronage.

People who moved to Crosby to take up a new business or vacant job in the community were interviewed for a story with their picture and a short biography—whether it was the single Colorado woman joining the staff of the Fish and Wildlife Service or a Minnesota family managing a new clothing store. School board and city council meetings were taken seriously and covered thoroughly . . .

Getting the local paper on Wednesday was clearly a highlight of the week to many. They looked forward to the front-page stories, certainly, and to John's outspoken views on many subjects in his weekly column . . . A (usually female) "correspondent" from each town listed who had sipped coffee with whom during the last week, and duly noted any out-of-town folks who had visited local relatives for a few days, including whether they made June-berry jam or pitched in with farm chores. Such items often prompted a belly-laugh back home among some of the out-of-state visitors unaccustomed to getting their name in a newspaper.

These local "columnists" were not ashamed of the simplicity of their news, but rather took pride in being able to "report" who had gone to what meeting, or how Mrs. O— was recovering from a bad fall on the ice—in short, what was happening in the lives of the people important to them—their own families, neighbors, relatives, friends (personal correspondence, 24 Jan. 1983).

Boerman writes of a way of life common to many millions of Americans, although strange to many more. What she describes is a tested way of chronicling. Historians carefully search through these kinds of newspapers when writing biographies of people who grew up in small towns in order to get clues about their activities and families. And as Boerman noted when she went to Williston, a relative metropolis of about fifteen thousand population, "I found it much easier to depend on the stories that were handed to me via public government bodies than to take the time to get to know the people in the community or to devise some way to keep track of the myriad of changes taking place with the oil boom. The requirements of each day left little time for reflecting on the historical perspectives of daily events" (ibid.).

The coverage in Pierre and Crosby obviously would be impossible in a large city. But the metropolitan reporter can learn much from Mrs. McNeill and Ms. Boerman. There is a profound human need for a feeling of community, to which journalists ought to be responsive. Wayne Stayskal, former Pulitzer prize-winning cartoonist for the *Chicago Tribune*, noted that neighborhoods in Chicago "are so varied that they really become separate communities with their own sets of 'news items' which are of no interest to outsiders. So to all these communities, the Chicago news can be as 'foreign' as any of the outside stuff" (personal correspondence, 19 Jan. 1983). Some newspapers devote columns and vignettes to what is happening in neighborhoods in their city. Others have set up special sections for various neighborhoods. A whole new group of suburban newspapers has sprung up in Washington, Chicago, and other cities.

Beyond the need for community, ingenious journalists can use stories about people—instead of institutions—to make their material come alive and take on relevance for the reader or listener. Professor of Journalism Walter H. Brovald of the University of Minnesota writes that the journalist ought to seize

... opportunities to tell stories in terms of *people.* Not just feature stories, but stories of complex issues and impersonal institutions; especially those, because issues and institutions, in the last analysis, *are* people and they are best understood in terms of people. It is one thing to write about the "drug problem"; it is quite another to report on a mother's reactions to her son's being convicted and sent to jail for a drug-related crime. It is one thing to write a story which discusses the increase in single, teenage mothers; it is something else to approach the problem through a single teenager willing to share the various facets of her experience.[6]

Russ Pulliam, columnist and editorial writer for the *Indianapolis News*, agrees. "The powerful are certainly newsworthy, but we tend to give them a kind of respect and reverence that they just don't get from God," Pulliam says. "We must work harder at writing about the little person, the one who is unique and unusual, yet not apparently powerful or important by the world's definition" (personal correspondence, 17 Jan. 1983). Pulliam has done just that. Quoting an Indiana Department of Public Instruction consultant who estimated that the average father spends thirty-six seconds a day in "positive interaction" with his child, Pulliam wrote about an Indiana state representative who was not seeking reelection because he wanted to spend more time with his family.

Paulette Pippert Cott says that the competition for news space is great and that when the Kansas legislature was in session, more than half of the stories on the air and in the paper were state house reports. Despite such competition, she was able to do such sensitive stories as a seven-segment series on child abuse. She interviewed a mother who had abused her daughter and was undergoing treatment in hopes of getting her child back. "She finally did," Mrs. Cott said. "The series won recognition from my peers as well as those working with abused children and abusive parents" (personal correspondence).

Mrs. Cott's remarks point up the problem of applying the personal dimension to the news. It is a difficult but essential task. One must be sensitive to people and what affects them. Craig Heaps, also a news broadcaster, comments:

> My feeling is that one of the highest responsibilities is to give people information upon which they can base decisions that affect their daily lives. Those decisions may be about who will govern, how they will spend their money, where they will be able to travel safely, or any of the infinite number of other decisions that come in living every day.[7]

A word of caution: Anecdotes and sidebars are effective in telling a story, but they should not become a substitute for hard, tough reporting of facts and even statistics. One should also guard against trivialities and the "cutesy" style.

## The Multidimensional Perspective

One of the most creative ideas for putting more perspective into stories was launched by Robert Kieckhefer while he was editor of the *Huron* (S.D.) *Daily Plainsman,* a major newspaper in South Dakota. He put a full-length, two-column essay entitled "Today's World" on page one every day. On one day, it dealt with international events; the second day, with federal matters; the third, with state news; the fourth, with sports; and the last day, with cultural matters. As UPI state manager, I wrote the state essay, about fifteen hundred words. I was allowed to treat a topic in depth each week. On one occasion, my subject was the eleven-point improvement goal adopted by the State Board of Education. One essay concerned the state librarian's plan to make books available in difficult, inaccessible areas of the far-flung prairie state. Another dealt with the Army Engineers' appraisal procedure, highly controversial with ranchers, in taking land for Missouri River dams and reservoirs. Still another concerned the shortage of technical staff in the State Health Department; another, the heavy toll from forest fires in the Black Hills; and another told why pheasants, a favorite game bird, are hungry. In the course of a year or so, I was able to write in depth on matters affecting almost every South Dakotan.

Historian John Rosselli of the University of Sussex in Brighton, England, once wrote:

> "Journalistic" in the university world means sloppy, hasty, ready to deal in slogans and half truths, brushing aside qualifications, sacrificing accuracy to brightness. In some ways this dislike is justified. Even if you're a serious journalist you often have to write in a hurry, you can't check everything, you dictate down the telephone, words get misheard, lines or whole paragraphs get cut at the last moment to make the story fit into the page . . .
>
> Yet the best of our serious journalists can beat many academics on their own ground—and sometimes do. They can unravel a complicated story as it's going on, apply critical thought to the issues it raises, and come up with something that's not only readable but that helps you to understand what had until then seemed blank or obscure . . .
>
> What the best journalists achieve in the everyday run of work is, I suggest, good reporting. It's still the heart of the profession. Reporting means to go out and look into what most people don't know about, or what they've heard about but don't understand, or what they see every day but overlook, and then come back to make it known. It means telling a story that enlightens. The rest is whipped cream.[8]

In order to go beyond the breaking development to write with depth and perspective, a news organization need not have superior resources, but only be more creative and persistent. Steve Bell, former anchorman on ABC's "Good Morning America," points out that hard news can be used as a peg to delve into trends. He writes:

> Ironically, ABC had early strength in that area in the late '60s and early '70s because we couldn't afford to get crews to the scene of many overseas breaking stories. To compensate, we would try to identify trends and potentially explosive stories, go in ahead of time, and package several sidebars to wait for the peg. If I were back on the local scene, I'm sure I would try to get more perspective into coverage through the sidebar approach. Yes, cover the hard news generated by basic trends, but also take advantage of the opportunity to help those caught in such "local" stories to step back and be aware of the larger context (personal correspondence, 24 Jan. 1983).

The wire services, with bureaus in evey state capital and many major cities, are uniquely able to write with perspective through "round-up" stories, that is, stories written in one bureau based on information supplied from several bureaus. UPI wrap-up weather reports traditionally are written by the Chicago bureau, based on messages and stories from bureaus where bad weather is occurring. But the formula can be used in countless ways. For instance, while I was a Chicago and Washington bureau desker, with easy access to other bureaus by means of the wire, I wrote:

> —A 1965 series on the major common issues facing state legislatures throughout the nation. The four dispatches revealed that the major issues were reapportionment, education and finance. Each story was filled with specific details from various states.
> —A 1971 series on the progress on county-city mergers in the United States. There were details on the post-World War II mergers of Miami-Dade County, Fla.; Nashville-Davidson County, Tenn.; Indianapolis-Marion County, Ind.; and others, as well as details on how and why Tampa-Hillsborough, Fla.; Chattanooga-Hamilton County, Tenn.; St. Louis-St. Louis County, Mo.; Memphis-Shelby County, Tenn.; Albuquerque-Bernalillo County, N.M.; and other cities and counties had rejected mergers.
> —A 1972 series on Roman Catholic education. It revealed that from parochial elementary schools up to seminaries, there were fewer institutions, falling enrollments, and financial problems. Often fundamentalist colleges, previously housed in poor facilities, bought magnificent Catholic campuses and moved into them. Again, there were specifics.

Each of the series lent itself to client newspapers writing a "local" angle to provide even more breadth to the story. Depth can be provided in individual stories as well as in series. When the House passed the most significant maritime legislation of the century, it was important to write later in greater detail, explaining that the new law would affect ocean-going ships as well as those on the Great Lakes and that it would encourage production of sleek, swift, capsule-carrying ships as contrasted to present-day ships that must be loaded and unloaded piece by piece. After Congress enacted the new mine safety law, a follow-up was important later to see how effective enforcement had been and what inspections had revealed.

Perhaps the in-depth stories that gave me the greatest satisfaction had little to do with government at all. These concerned the droughts that hit the Dakotas, often scorching the prairie grass and spring wheat by May and dashing the ranchers' hopes for another year.

One story began:

> Pierre, S.D.—The double-barreled 1955 drought, the prolonged fall and winter feeding season and lack of moisture this year have combined to present one of the most discouraging pictures to ranchers and farmers in South Dakota in two decades.
>
> South Dakota old-timers are saying the drought and hot spell this spring and summer are "almost parallel" to the dry "dust bowl" years of the 1930s.
>
> But State Secretary of Agriculture Charles Bruett of Pierre says that all hope is not lost . . .

A few years later, another drought hit the prairie, and this time, I took a different tack. I wrote a series of three dispatches. One focused on the immediate impact and eventual effect of the dry spell. The second estimated that the loss was running into the hundreds of thousands of dollars. For the third, I contacted a prominent minister and a Sioux Falls psychiatrist to see how the people were handling it. With a sort of "hope springs eternal" attitude, they said.

CHAPTER 4

# *Justice, Peace, Morality*

## JUSTICE AND PEACE

The ethical reporter who is committed to truth will inevitably be drawn in whatever story he or she is covering to the dimensions of justice, peace, and morality, for the dynamic of truth yields justice and peace. As I assert elsewhere, the issues of justice are clear in the Occupied West Bank of Israel or in civil rights matters. But issues of justice are equally present on the sports beat, the society page, the business section, and farm news. Reporters on these beats may simply have to dig deeper.

This does not mean that the reporter plays an advocacy role on a day-to-day basis. It does mean, however, that the journalist is alert and sensitive to stories involving justice or injustice—stories that, if they were only covered, would meet the traditional standards of newsworthiness and legitimacy. The mass media must take note of wrong and oppressive conditions in our society and write stories for the express purpose of bringing about justice and peace. Obviously, this must be done with careful discernment and judgment.

Walter Brovald of the University of Minnesota has written, "It is interesting that in every extended discussion I have had with groups or individual students, a discussion of journalistic ethics as a practical matter has ended up in terms of justice, fairness, and a concern for others."[1]

Justice starts at home. The paucity of blacks and Spanish-speaking people in the mass media, especially in positions of leadership, reveals another kind of racism. The American Society of Newspaper Editors' 1988 employment survey showed that 7.02 percent of the newsroom work force is made up of black, Hispanic, Asian and American Indian professionals—less than half their proportion of the population at large. The survey did show improvement, however, up from 6.56 percent in 1987.[2]

It is possible, even imperative, for the journalist to find issues of justice in such unlikely beats as sports, agriculture or society. As for the society page: Is it right that in some major cities with a predominantly black population, most of the social items in the daily papers are still about whites?

My three-year assignment in the Middle East brought truth, justice and peace together in a profound triumvirate. There was a confluence of the main currents of my life—a concern for justice, the Judeo-Christian tradition with its origins in the Land of the Bible, the excitement of covering one of the biggest ongoing news stories of our time. There were the issues of the endless quest for peace between the Arabs and the Jews, of justice for Palestinians who find themselves living under Israeli control, of finding truth in a Mediterranean culture in which exaggeration and emotion often obscure the facts. One foreign correspondent, not an American, told me that his principal concern in covering Israel was to do travelogues.

During her triumphant visit to the United States, Philippine President Corazon Aquino spoke on the role the press played in the Philippine revolution and touched upon "The reality that you, more than others, should recognize: the liberating virtue of truth and the power of the media to make it happen."[3]

As a newly arrived reporter in South Dakota in the late 1950s, I soon discovered that the state had one of the largest Indian populations in proportion to the general population of any state in the Union: one in twenty-eight South Dakotans was an Indian. Many lived on reservations. Since reservations are federal land, offenders on the reservations were sent to *federal* prisons. Considering that thirty-four percent of the population at the *state* penitentiary were Indians who had committed off-reservation crimes, one can begin to comprehend the problem of law enforcement among the Indians. I wrote a broadcast story for national distribution pointing out these facts and citing examples of several Indians who had committed crimes. The main problem, the U.S. attorney said, was that "ninety to ninety-five percent of the crime on the reservation is traceable to intoxicating liquor." I concluded, "The penalty comes stiffer for Indians than it does for the white man. Most Indians . . . penniless . . . waive hearings, enter a plea and are sentenced within a short period of time. Seldom does one have sufficient funds to post bond or hire a lawyer to defend himself."

During my six years in the Dakotas, the plight of the Indians never left my awareness. When I arrived there, Indian traffic victims were identified as such. Whites were not racially identified. When this practice is repeated scores of times, the strong implication is that Indians are bad drivers. I ended the practice of racial identification.

Previously, homicides on Indian reservations were treated with only a few paragraphs, while coverage of white slayings was blown up. This implied that lives of Indians were not as valuable as those of whites. Barring other factors such as the victim's or suspect's fame, I handled homicides of Indians and whites the same way. When the U.S. Civil Rights Commission held hearings on the Rosebud Reservation, I covered them personally, wrote in detail about them, and followed up later with analytic stories.

Using the access of a wire service to newspapers throughout the nation, in later assignments I continued to publicize the plight of the Indians. In 1963, as a UPI Chicago editor, I filed in our "editor's schedule" a dispatch about the South Dakota attorney general, who called hearings to determine whether policemen chained Indian prisoners and took liberties with Indian women. Later, in Washington, although it was not my beat, I tried to write stories on what was happening at the seldom-reported Bureau of Indian Affairs.

All of these were newsworthy stories. They did not violate traditional journalistic standards of what is news and what is not. But they added a critical dimension of justice.

About nine years after I halted the practice of racial identification of traffic victims, the UPI Log, which was distributed weekly to UPI staffers, stated the rule: "If you identify a person as to race, color or creed, have reason for it." The log pointed out that one exception might be a crime where "there seems to be no question that the identification of a wanted suspect as black, white or yellow is as much a part of his description as whether he is short or tall, fat or slim." Another exception was in the Middle East, where Jews and Arabs visit so much injustice on each other for no other reason than their racial indentities. Here, I believe, the publication of the racial identities can help expose this injustice.

Numerous groups in our society are underprivileged or oppressed: blacks, Hispanic Americans, small religious colonies such as the Hutterites in South Dakota, migrant workers, patients in institutions for the mentally ill and mentally retarded, the poor, and prisoners. And beyond our shores are the developing nations, known as the Third World or the Southern Hemisphere. The list is far from complete. All ought to compel the journalist's attention.

The mass media often cover only a breaking development, a congressional hearing, or a news conference announcing a study—and drop the story there. We need to keep going back to the story again and again. In this way the issues of justice and mercy often are revealed. More will probably be accomplished through ongoing stories, even small ones, than by one big takeout. H.L. Stevenson, former UPI editor-in-chief, once remarked to me that perhaps it was more important to go back the second and third day to find out why a riot occurred in Chicago's South Side slums than merely to report that it occurred.

I believe the story itself has the power to bring justice. Even without being an advocate, merely by reporting the situation and exposing it to the light of truth, the journalist becomes an agent of justice. The problem with blatant advocacy journalism is that its practitioners often suffer the fatal flaw of writing in a strident style. Rather than being effective, they lose credibility and perhaps even harm the cause they are espousing.

One dispatch I wrote concerned the fifteen thousand Hutterites in South Dakota, an industrious, God-fearing people who had emigrated from Russia in the 1870s. Federal mental health studies showed that divorce, suicide, insanity, juvenile delinquency and drunkenness were almost unknown among Hutterites and that they were among the "happiest, most well-adjusted groups in the world." But outsiders felt threatened when the Hutterites began buying land to expand their beautiful barns and fields. They were prosperous but had little concern for amassing money. They were able to buy surrounding farm land because they would pay any price a neighbor asked. Their foes shouted "Communism!" The 1955 state legislature passed a law declaring it illegal for a communal corporation to expand. Eventually, the Hutterites took their case to the state Supreme Court. The court let the specific purchase of land stand, but ruled the ban on expansion was constitutional.

As a cycle editor in the Chicago and Washington UPI bureaus in following years, I tried to be alert to similar stories. The early and mid-1960s in Chicago were the period of open housing demonstrations and school desegregation controversies, and there were frequent opportunities to write stories about them for national distribution. The late 1960s were a time of racial upheaval throughout the nation; and there were daily occasions for "ed sked" stories, particularly stories that went below the surface to respond to the kind of continuing concern that H.L. Stevenson expressed.

It is my contention that the mere reporting of these events—that is, exposing them to the light of truth—helped achieve a new measure of justice in the land. Calling these matters to the people's attention helped raise their consciousness. I believe most people want to be fair and their awareness of these things forced the president, Congress, governors, legislators and local officials to administer justice.

Spanish-speaking people, constituting between five and ten percent of our population, are another group that the mass media have largely ignored. Yet the story opportunities are there. Here are a couple from my own experience:

WASHINGTON—The Equal Employment Opportunity Commission's study of Spanish-surnamed Americans reveals "a caste system" (1970).

WASHINGTON—The Spanish-speaking have given the word to both parties: Latinos may hold the balance in a close election in at least four big states and they had better be given their due consideration (1972).

Many migrant workers are Spanish-speaking people who engage in hard "stoop" labor that most people would refuse to do. Their plight led to a series of congressional hearings conducted by then-Sen. Walter F. Mondale, D-Minn. Few news agencies covered them over a period of time. Again, it was important to keep pursuing the story.

WASHINGTON—The director of a two-year research project on migrant workers in America said Friday the Yuba City, Calif., mass slayings show they are "nameless, faceless" people whose plight is one of the nation's most serious problems.

Another story dealt with the deplorable living conditions of migrant workers in Texas and Florida. Every one of fourteen hundred persons tested had dental problems; many children under twelve had ear defects; migrant workers suffered the only polio deaths in the nation that year; one case of leprosy was even reported.

In South Dakota, I wrote special stories on the patients at the Redfield State Hospital for the mentally retarded; on conditions at Yankton State Hospital for the mentally ill; on teenagers at the coed Plankinton State Training Center. The Plankinton story was particularly fascinating. The center had no restraints or locked doors, and a psychiatrist said this presented a terrible dilemma for errant teenagers who knew they could walk away any time they wished. This temptation does not confront the prison inmate, who knows that "the wall" is there, with guards and trained rifles atop it.

Russ Pulliam of the *Indianapolis News* has written extensively about penal reform, often quoting Charles W. Colson, former Nixon White House lawyer and now, in William F. Buckley's view, one of the foremost twentieth century experts on prison reform. Pulliam confesses: "I have written a lot on this subject and have won awards for it, but I still don't think I have adequately told the story of the poor and the black in Indianapolis."

Paulette Pippert Cott, a news broadcaster, has told of the personal cost in such assignments. "In covering the courthouse, I never reported on anything less than the 'violent' crimes." she writes. "There were times I came out of court, trying to write a story with tears in my eyes. It was difficult watching the families of the victim and the defendant deal with their emotions. Perhaps another sidebar if there is time. It had to be done. People want to know that the judicial system is fair, that it does not just get the rich, who can afford the high-priced attorneys, off the hook. They also want to know their community is safe, that those who commit a crime will be rightfully punished and will not be a threat to their families" (personal correspondence).

Opportunities for this kind of story are more plentiful at the local level than at the national. I found this to be true in comparing my experience in the Dakotas with that in Chicago, Washington and Jerusalem. While covering the Carter White House, I wrote about the impact of President Carter's human rights policy. After being assigned to Congress at the start of the Reagan administration, I conceived and carried out a five-part series on how domestic budget cuts would affect the quality of life for Americans in the areas of health, education, welfare and jobs. As part of the series, I wrote one fifteen hundred-word dispatch for each area on the legislative aspect, and then got one of our bureaus in key regions to write an accompanying story—a sidebar—in terms of a family or local situation. Washington stories can sketch the legislative and legal aspects, but local newspapers and stations can best describe the situation in vivid personal terms.

Stories involving injustice do not lack newsworthiness, but members of the mass media often show insensitivity and lack of awareness toward them.

## MORALITY

Based on my own major assignments of recent years—the 1972 McGovern presidential campaign, the Watergate scandal, the Carter campaigns and presidency, Congress, and the Middle East, I have concluded that the mass media often are incompetent, uneasy or unwilling to deal with the moral dimension of public issues. I do not mean by this such so-called "moral" questions as abortion, pornography, and sexual misdeeds; rather, I am talking about traits of character that public officials reveal in situations that shape decision making and the course of events. I am referring to the classical virtues of courage and loyalty, to how the official defines and uses power, to one's mind set or world view. We often fail to probe these things, and by our failure we do not serve truth.

During the 1976 campaign, I once asked Jody Powell, who was Carter's chief spokesman and interpreter throughout the 1970s, how he felt the press had handled Carter's religious experience. He replied: "The American people, as a whole, are probably better equipped to understand that aspect of Jimmy Carter's life than are the people who are trying to explain it to them. The coverage has been mixed. There have been stories that have been superficial and slipshod and biased to the extreme, not against him but based on what I take to be a general distaste for religious faith" (personal interview aboard the campaign plane).

I am not saying we ought to convert news stories into religious tracts or advocacy declarations. But I am saying that we miss a vital dimension to the news if we scoff at or skip over morality or justice or faith when it is an essential part of the story. Obviously, this is a big challenge. We need to be able to report and write about morality without moralizing. We need to understand what we are writing about. We must use words in such a way that they mean the same thing to the reader or viewer as they mean to the person who spoke to them. This task belongs on the agenda of academic journalists, and it ought to be in the awareness of every editor and news director. It surely should be on the mind of all of us who constitute the working press, in our pursuit of truth.

Dr. Clifford G. Christians, who teaches media ethics and social philosophy of communications at the University of Illinois, has offered a structure for the ethical training of journalists. Christians suggests studying Aristotle, Hume and Kant, who demonstrate three classical ways of constructing an ethical system.[4] Or, he suggests choosing explicit ethical orientations, such as humanism (strong values but without religious commitment), Judeo-Christianity, utilitarianism (whatever works most effectively, decided case by case), or positivism (social convention determines values). He also sets forth the goals in teaching journalism ethics: (1) to enable the journalist to recognize ethical issues, (2) to develop analytical skills, (3) to stimulate the moral imagination, and (4) to elicit moral obligation.

Perhaps the simplest method is best. The journalist who wants to be more ethically and morally sensitive can do so simply by asking a person who has reflected or written on the ethical implications of the issue.

Russ Pulliam of the *Indianapolis News* follows this less academic approach. "I think I have been able to identify a cultural decline in America in some of my columns, along with prescriptions seldom offered in the secular news media, bringing to public attention writers like Francis Schaeffer, Elton Trueblood, Charles Malik ... " (personal correspondence).

While covering the Watergate scandal, I frequently used the sidewalk news conferences outside the U.S. District Courthouse in Washington to ask Watergate defendants whether they felt remorse. Their negative or blasé answers often revealed much about the moral climate of the Nixon administration. As a reporter in South Dakota, I drove several hundred miles to hear and interview anthropologist Margaret Mead and David Elton Trueblood, a Quaker theologian. I interviewed Iowa farmer Roswell Garst a few years after his famous encounter with Nikita Krushchev. I interviewed Carl F.H. Henry on why the evangelical community has become more socially conscious. I interviewed Pete Dawkins on the role of heroes in America. Each of these persons offered moral points of view not frequently seen in news stories.

Dawkins had been my hero since boyhood because of his exploits at West Point; he was 1957 Heisman trophy winner, an All-America football halfback, president of his class, first captain of the corps and a Rhodes scholar. Later, he received an interdisciplinary doctorate at Princeton.

I interviewed him several times. The first time, in 1972, I asked him, for no particular reason, how much over his playing weight he was. "I'm at my playing weight," he said, demonstrating his remarkable discipline.

At the time of my second interview, we were in his office in one of the Pentagon's inner rings at the very moment the Air Florida flight piled into the 14th Street Bridge a short distance away during a January 1982 blizzard. By now, Dawkins was the Army's youngest brigadier general, ahead of schedule toward becoming Army Chief of Staff, a post predicted for him while he was at West Point. He was wearing a simple black sweater (and was now five pounds *under* his playing weight). His colleagues called him "Pete." Since I knew little about military science, I wasn't certain exactly what direction the interview would take. Somehow, it turned to heroes.

"It's terribly important to have heroes," Dawkins told me. "A lot of things that are really central parts of our lives are transcendent or abstract. But it's hard for us to deal with courage or dedication or sacrifice in the abstract. We need to have people who embody those qualities, people who are reassuring and real ...

"Yet much as we need them and want them, we're somehow not comfortable with heroes. No culture ever has been, I suppose. Even the Greeks, who 'invented' heroes, cast them out. But we seem to turn on ours with special fervor, driven by an almost compulsive need to scratch and rub anyone of heroic dimension until we find a wart or blemish. We microscopically examine people in public life until we find something about them that is flawed. Only then do we seem content to let them be. Curious, isn't it?"[5]

# CHAPTER 5

# The Power of the Press

The popular view is that the front pages of a daily newspaper provide the news and information, and the editorial pages contain opinions and attempts to influence the reader. The truth actually may be the reverse of this. The real influence-wielding may be in the front section of the newspaper, not in the content of the stories but rather in their selection.

## TO INFLUENCE

When it was officially disclosed that certain senators were earning huge sums in lecture fees, the press responded with vigorous coverage. In the public outcry that followed, the Senate enacted a measure to limit the amount of fees each senator could earn.

One of the biggest earners, Sen. Jake Garn, R-Utah, arose during the heated debate and shouted, "Maybe that is one of the big problems today: We are so intimidated by the press, the all-powerful press, who sit back and disclose nothing, tell nothing, and then get a bee in their bonnet—'Boy, are they going to get it!' They write a few editorials and some of us panic and run or are intimidated" (Senate floor, June 9, 1983).

Vice President Spiro T. Agnew reflected this same opinion of the press in his November 1969 speeches aimed at the media. Speaking of television, he said: "No medium has more profound influence over public opinion. Nowhere in our system are there fewer checks on vast power." Many people, like Garn and Agnew, believe that the press is powerful and do not hesitate to say so. They assume that the press deliberately controls, manipulates, and shapes public opinion. "In the popular view, mass communication exerts tremendous political influence," one researcher wrote.[1]

Others are more blunt. "The public does not believe that the leaders of our institutions and our government are really as dumb or corrupt as they appear in the press," said Herbert Schmertz, Mobil public affairs vice president and a press critic. "Nor do they believe the institutions of our society are as rotten and uncaring as they are portrayed."[2]

In similar fashion, some people, often highly placed, believe the press is responsible for changing morals. Pope John Paul II warned of the manipulation of the human mind by "social communication media." He did not single out the electronic media or exclude the press, but it was clear that he was aiming at television. These media, he said, "penetrate into the intimacy of the home and reach the most humble and distant places. They offer many advantages: They inform quickly, they teach, they entertain, make all men brothers, they combine rational expression and image, symbols and personal contact. The word is complemented by esthetic and artistic expression . . . Their power is such that they give strength to what they mention while diminishing what they omit."[3]

This assumption that the mass media have huge power requires a low view of human beings, a view that they can be manipulated by what they read in the newspaper or see on a TV newscast. It also calls to mind the king who held the messenger accountable for the bad news he brought and killed him.

Gerald Priestland offered an effective rebuttal to this assumption when he said, "I believe, and this is surely in keeping with the Christian doctrine of free will, that people are a great deal less malleable than they are thought to be."[4] "Certainly I have never had the experience of meeting a listener or reader who complained he had been tricked by the media into voting the wrong way. But I have met plenty who were convinced that other, less perceptive, voters had been so deceived," Priestland said, only partly tongue in cheek.[5]

Numerous polls demonstrated that about twenty-five percent of the people felt that Richard Nixon was hounded out of office. Obviously, people did not believe what they heard reported in the media about Watergate, or at least they were not influenced by it. If the twenty-five percent figure represents the hard core of people deeply cynical about the press and therefore suspicious of its power, then certainly a much larger percentage have doubts of some kind about the media. Jimmy Carter, from rural South Georgia, was elected governor in 1970 without the support of the state's newspapers. Ralph Yarborough, a liberal

Democrat, won three elections to the U.S. Senate from Texas, where the newspapers were so hostile that they all but unanimously opposed him and often refused even to carry stories about him. George McGovern, another liberal Democrat, won three elections as senator from South Dakota, despite the hostility of the state's newspapers.

If the media are so powerful in controlling opinion, how were Carter, Yarborough, McGovern and many others who did not enjoy the support of the press, able to win?

Benjamin C. Bradlee, executive editor of the *Washington Post,* one of the nation's top newspapers, took a cynical view when he was asked how powerful he was. "I don't know . . . Everybody tells me that I'm powerful. But I can't get the trash collected. I mean, if I try to exert any real power around here the way it is exerted by 'powerful' people in America, I'd be laughed out of town."[6]

The real power of the press is not its ability to shape or control opinion. Rather, the real power of the press lies in its selection of the stories for its audience and in setting the "agenda" for them. These are assertions to which I shall return.

Let us tarry for a moment, however, on the matter of the power of the press to influence. Ironically, if the press wields such power, it probably exerts it more on the powerful than on the powerless—that is to say, more on the politicians than on the people. This is why politicians are so eager to appear on the networks' morning or Sunday talk shows.

Bernard Hennessy says the "common knowledge" that the mass media influence elections, legislation and executive decisions "is especially cherished by defeated candidates and reformist groups who find some comfort in the identification of scapegoats for the failures of their causes."[7]

The journalist and the politician maintain a symbiotic relationship of mutual envy and awe. "The journalist is fascinated by power, the politician by communication, and neither can do without the other," Priestland says.[8] "Quite simply . . . political decisionmakers often *think* they [the media] are important," Hennessy affirms. "Political actors tend to believe that the mass media have insight into the 'public mind' (an illusion carefully nurtured by the self-image of the press)."

A British researcher, Colin Seymour-Ure, contends that the mistake of overestimating the power of newspapers over their readers "arises largely from a misconception about what people think newspapers are for. The reasons why people read newspapers at all and why they read one paper instead of another have practically nothing to do with politics." He continues, "The political opinions of newspapers, moreover, are a very minor factor in attracting or repelling readers. . . . In brief, they are one of the many things which, over a long period of time, shape a person's attitudes toward his society and its political institutions and machinery."[10]

In like manner, people generally do not watch television to gain political insights. "What they really want," Priestland says, "is entertainment and escape, not intellectual stimulation."[11]

Seymour-Ure describes three distinctions in analyzing the impact of the press. First, at the bottom of the list, an item makes an impact if it is remembered or stimulates thought. Second, an item has an impact if it changes or reinforces the reader's attitudes or opinions. Third, and most significant, an item has impact if it produces not just a change of opinion but also a change of action, as in voting behavior.[12] This third power is probably much less operative than many people assume.

"It is impossible to do more than guess about the influence of newspapers on changing attitudes to drugs, capital punishment, chastity, divorce and so on in any generation," Seymour-Ure concludes. "On the other hand, it is very difficult to be altogether skeptical and discard the hypothesis that newspapers by virtue simply of being one of the means of mass communication in our society, do have some, albeit unquantifiable, influence over our general *mores*."[13]

If the press affects public opinion at all, it apparently does so through the technique of reinforcement. Researchers agree that the mass media do not generally change an individual's existing political attitudes, values and beliefs, but reinforce those feelings. Richard M. Merelman comments: "The explanation for this phenomenon lies, to a large extent, in cognitive dissonance theory which states that individuals tend to pay more attention to the mass-media messages with which they agree than those with which they disagree."[14]

The press also has a power that is negative in nature: the television error that is gone forever into the air, the newspaper correction that seldom catches the eye of the person who reads the initial mistake.

The communications industry varies from medium to medium in affecting the reader or viewer. In the simplest terms, the wire service, operating on a deadline every minute, can provide the score, the death toll, the outcome of the election, the markets. The daily newspaper can provide a bit more detail, but not much. The weekly news magazine provides the news of the day, often with "an angle." The monthly journal can provide analysis. Excepting the so-called "instant" books that are little more than expanded magazine articles, it takes a book to put something into ultimate perspective. The most influential of the media, Priestland says, is a book.

Television, on the other hand, has the immediacy of the wire sevices and the power of a picture. Priestland confesses that he is skeptical of the supposed power of his own medium, television. It is particularly prone to the media's persistent superficiality.[15]

There is often a powerful authenticity in the picture flashed on the TV screen. In this writer's opinion, the Watergate investigation, despite the heroics of two newspaper reporters, would never have succeeded were it not for the televising of the 1973 Senate Watergate hearings. Day after day, the people could watch John W. Dean III's expressions and judge for themselves as he made charges of criminality against the Nixon administration. They were able to look at and listen to John Mitchell, John Ehrlichman, H.R. Haldeman, and others making their protestations and denials. The people knew they were hearing testimony first-hand and not merely depending on news stories that faceless, often nameless reporters had written. In this case, the perception of reality far outweighed the superficiality of television. Similarly, Sen. J. William Fulbright's Foreign Relations Committee's televised hearings in 1966 on the Vietnam war were a major factor in turning public opinion against the conflict. Once again, the audience could hear the testimony first-hand and evaluate it knowledgeably without having the testimony filtered through a reporter's computer.

Angus Campbell, the University of Michigan pollster, has said that televised coverage of political campaigning "has succeeded in making a sizeable part of the electorate direct witnesses to episodes in recent political history."[16] But he adds, "It seems neither to have elevated the general level of political interest nor to have broadened the total range of political information."[17]

According to Gallup polls, 72 percent of the public in 1985 and 71 percent in 1986 thought news organizations were highly professional and only 11 percent in 1985 and 13 percent in 1986 thought the media were not professional. But only 34 percent of the public in 1985 and 37 percent in 1986 thought that news organizations presented news about political and social issues fairly. More than half—53 percent in 1985 and 57 percent in 1986—thought the media favored one side.[18]

The power of the press is probably greater in smaller communities than in large ones for the simple reason that people tend to be more suspicious of the distant and remote, and more trusting of what is close at hand. Spiro Agnew and others exploited this sentiment during the Nixon administration by engendering hostility toward the so-called "Eastern Establishment liberal press" and the "Boston-New York-Washington axis" of controlled news. Said Agnew: "A small group of men, numbering perhaps no more than a dozen anchormen, commentators, and executive producers . . . decide what 40 to 50 million Americans will learn of the day's events ... To a man these commentators and producers live and work in the geographical and intellectual confines of Washington, D.C., or New York City."[19]

Agnew did not contend that this select group were born or educated in Washington and New York. Of the network anchormen, Dan Rather was born and educated in Texas, Tom Brokaw of NBC was born and educated in South Dakota, and Peter Jennings of ABC is a Canadian. On the important morning shows, Bryant Gumbel of the NBC "Today" show is the son of a Chicago judge and cohost Jane Pauley was born and educated in Indiana; Joan Lunden of ABC's "Good Morning America" is a Californian and cohost Charles Gibson is a native of the Middle West. Of all these, only Gumbel and Gibson were educated in the East. Maybe Agnew really meant that the real control spot for network news is the Middle West.

Ironically, the local editor, whom many townspeople probably know and like, may be much more likely to participate in a Watergate-type cover-up than an editor in a large city. In a small town, the police chief, editor and big merchant on Main Street may be close pals. An embarrassing story would be much more likely to be exposed in a large city, where competition would force an editor to run a story about even a close friend.

Competition is a spur to more aggressive news coverage, but in many cities such competition is waning. Although the total number of daily newspapers in the United States is holding almost steady, there are more and more major cities with only one daily. From 1946 to 1987, the number of dailies merely dropped from 1,763 to 1,645. The number of papers with under 50,000 circulation dropped from 1,564 to 1,394; with circulation over 250,000 rose from 38 to 39. These statistics may not seem ominous, but among the 1,526 cities with a daily newspaper, only 44 cities had at least two separately owned newspapers. The 44 included 19 cities where newspapers were published under joint ownership agreement, in which the newspapers shared some noneditorial functions.[20] John Morton, a newspaper analyst, has said that these days the history of starting a new newspaper is almost "nonexistent." A start-up will succeed "only if it is different enough to create a market" (personal interview, February 1987).

One of the most significant developments among daily newspapers is the growth of chains, representing economic concentration of the print media. Gannett owned 89 daily newspapers in 1988, Knight-Ridder 30 papers, and Newhouse, 25; other growing groups have commercial control over scores of papers.[21]

There is more competition among television stations. Virtually every one of the largest 50 markets had four or more TV stations, and the next 100 largest had three or more. According to Chuck Sherman, senior vice president-television, National Association of Broadcasters, nearly every commercial TV station in the country has local competition. It is not clear, however, how many of these stations have full-time news staffs as do newspapers.

## IN SELECTION

The great power of the press lies in its prerogative to select the stories to be covered. This is an awesome power that cannot be minimized. Wire editors and television producers do not make spot checks of public opinion when choosing a story for one or another edition or news program. They rely on their own hunches and filters. Viewer and reader alike are at the mercy of the editor and producer as to what they may see on a page or in a newscast. The viewer and reader may not put much trust in the stories they are being given, but they have almost no say in the selection process.

An examination of front pages and network news programs shows that most editors and producers pick the same stories day after day. There is no blatant conspiracy in this. The network producers do not make a conference call each afternoon to see which stories to run that night. It is far more subtle and insidious. The editors and producers probably are white and middle class, have gone to similar colleges and universities, have covered the same beats on their way up the ladder, and talk to the same people—often each other. Is it any wonder that their decisions about which stories to use and how those stories will be used are so alike? The readers and viewers are hostages of the editor and producer. Often they do not even know about stories to which they have been denied access. The power of the press to select is troubling; the power of the press to omit is even more troubling.

The networks select the same stories with cookie-cutter monotony. This was confirmed by my own survey of news summaries prepared by the White House staff over a fifteen-month period. Every administration prepares for its top officials a daily White House summary, which includes a summary of the top news items of the day in various leading newspapers and the three networks' evening news programs. Bill Hart, director of the Reagan White House's news summary, said he included any story that might affect the administration. He deleted such stories as natural disasters or individual feats that probably did not require administration attention.

In thirty-six daily news summaries selected in a fifteen-month period in 1982-83, 191 of the top 342 news stories had been used by at least two of the networks. On seven days, all three networks led with the same two or three stories. What makes these figures more telling is that all networks probably would use a story about a great individual feat or a terrible natural disaster, and thus, the stories that were tabulated in the news summaries represented areas in which editors and producers could have used some ingenuity in selection—but did not.

Observes Gerald Priestland: "What seems to make editors happiest is to spread out all the morning's papers and broadcast transcripts on the office floor and to find that they all have the same stories in roughly the same order and with no contradictions."[22] "The wizards of public relations may plan and scheme, and may 'float' or 'balloon up' endless ideas, but their skills are for naught unless the city desk or the nightly news takes note. When an issue is picked up by the papers and TV news, a serious and sustained dialogue may take place . . . " Hennessy contends.[23]

Concludes Seymour-Ure: "Because newspapers can decide what to print and omit they are in a position of political power. Further, as well as being a 'neutral' channel, newspapers can press upon their readers their own views instead of leaving them to work out conclusions for themselves."[24]

What can the consumer do about this? As I said in chapter 2, the reader-viewer can go to more than one channel of information. This will help assure—although not guarantee, as discussed in the "cookie-cutter conformity" of the press—that more than one person has selected the reader-viewer's news menu. Catch Channel 9 news at six o'clock and Channel 4 at eleven. Compare the TV news with the daily newspaper. See what a journal of opinion is saying.

# In Agenda Setting

Another great power of the press lies in setting the agenda for public discussion. At the least, more than one conversation has been prompted by a story in the paper. A story in the morning newspaper about a controversy will not necessarily dictate how people feel about it, but the story will ignite discussion—and keep the issue alive. The *Washington Post*'s sustained coverage kept Watergate alive until finally the cover-up began to unravel nine months after the break-in, and the rest of the media were marshalled.

Despite Jake Garn's outburst against the press, reported earlier in this chapter, the Senate voted to impose limits on outside earned income. Sen. Henry M. Jackson, D-Wash., walked into the Senate radio-TV gallery and told reporters: "The press has done a good job. You zeroed in on the right thing ... honoraria, and properly so."

"[The press] may not be successful much of the time in telling people what to think, but it is stunningly successful in telling its readers what to think *about*," one researcher said.[25]

While covering the South Dakota State Capitol as a young reporter, I wandered into the office of State Comptroller John C. Penne. His office had been established to make unannounced spot checks on state and local officials. I did not know that the wire services—the only reporters who staffed the State House—usually ignored these audit reports unless Penne's sleuths found major skullduggery. The audit reports usually contained criticism of faulty practices and poor management that were not sufficiently serious to indicate prosecution. Innocently, I began to write stories about the criticisms found in these reports. Soon the AP began writing about them. Later, Penne told me that his audit reports generally had been ignored by the officials but when the public began to hear and read about them, the officials took notice and started correcting their ways. During the first year in which I wrote about those audit reports, a poll of broadcasters placed the stories as one of the top ten news stories of the year in South Dakota, and Penne was nominated as "man of the year."

As I wrote to my editor at the time: "There were pieces on the city councilmen at Rapid City who bought white dinner jackets with public funds, the small town west of the Missouri River that gave free light bulbs as a bonus for paying accounts; the municipal bartender at Eagle Butte who kept accepting worthless checks—even though he knew they would bounce—until he had a stack several inches high, etc."

Ben Bradlee spelled out in his *American Heritage* interview what the power of his newspaper is: "The power of the *Washington Post* lies mostly in its ability to focus national attention on certain subjects. If the editors of the *Post* think something's important, they can wheel up their firepower to concentrate on that subject." When the interviewer asked, "Who sets the agenda for the nation, the *Washington Post* and who else?" Bradlee replied, "*The New York Times* and the television networks and *Time* and *Newsweek*."[26]

Bradlee's reporters Bob Woodward and Carl Bernstein, by focusing a series of stories on Watergate, were finally able to rivet the nation's attention on that scandal. The crime had been committed, but not until the press selected it for coverage and made it an item on the daily agenda did the people find out the truth.

Yet, it is the primary function of the media to inform and define and point out, not to advocate, and this may be one reason why the press is not as persuasive as advertising. Marketing specialists consciously strive to court and change people's minds—to sell a product. The press' main commodity, as I have said, is truth, which is often unvarnished and lacking sparkle.

Often, so-called bad news can be used to set agenda. Coverage of tragedies may help bring reform. For example, at a 1983 congressional hearing, Washington Redskin place kicker Mark Mosely and Mrs. Roberta Roper testified about the brutal and sadistic slayings of members of their families. The story was given nationwide attention. Although many people find such grim accounts abhorrent, the news stories helped bring about changes in sentencing laws in Maryland and provided the legislative background for new federal sentencing legislation.

Says Priestland: "It is often possible to argue convincingly that the exposure of one case of abuse will alert the public to the existence of others."[27] He contends that people who discuss their case with the press may experience a personal catharsis. "Interviews with the bereaved are not always the heartless affairs you might suppose. People often want to talk about their loss or outrage . . . What may look like an intrusion into private grief may turn into a breaking out of it."[28]

# IN THE FUTURE

Technology has blurred and is still blurring the traditional definitions of the news media. With the advent of television throughout the nation after World War II, the visual aspects of the news were emphasized, giving new meaning to the old saying, "A picture is worth a thousand words."

Afternoon newspapers are suffering the most from this development, partly because of the harsh economics and logistics of publishing at the busiest hour of the day, partly because people began to get their suppertime news from the networks. Between 1946 and 1986, the number of PM newspapers dropped from 1,429 to 1,220.[29] PMers always have had a difficult time because they must be reported, edited, printed, hauled throughout the area, and home-delivered during peak, high-traffic daytime hours. As traffic increased, the deadlines had to be moved up earlier and earlier, until many afternoon newspapers have deadlines before anything of significance has happened during the day.

There are parallel problems for all the print media in the coverage of news. Press deadlines became increasingly early, but television deadlines became later and later as technology grew more sophisticated. Video tape replaced film, enabling a network to go to live coverage or to use video tape on an event only moments after it occurred. What could an afternoon newspaper report that would be news to the persons getting home from work in late afternoon and turning on slick, well-produced network news shows? What could an afternoon newspaper report that, as a matter of fact, had not already been in the morning newspaper? The front-pages of afternoon newspapers no longer resembled the traditional newspapers with a smattering of international, national, and local news; they began instead to concentrate on the feature approach, as did the ill-fated afternoon *Minneapolis Star*, or almost exclusively on local news, as did the *Mason City Globe-Gazette*.

"I think we all made some adjustments at first—in the '50s, early '60s—when we were convinced we had to find a way to 'fight' TV," says Charles Walk, editor of the *Bismarck* (N.D.) *Tribune*. "I believe, however, that most of us came to realize that the best way to battle the tube was to do a better job of what we were doing before it came along. The problem was that we tried to be like television. Then, we came back to the good, honest coverage that puts us ahead of them in all areas, except timeliness" (personal correspondence, 13 Jan. 1983).

The three major TV networks themselves ran into severe competition—from Ted Turner's all-news Cable News Network; from Pat Robertson's Christian Broadcasting Network; and from a dozen regional networks and cable competitors. Stanley S. Hubbard, headquartered in Minneapolis-St. Paul, organized a network of fifty-one affiliated stations that provided news coverage never before available to independent stations without network affiliation. Local stations, starting an assault on the networks, now send their own correspondents to Washington and even overseas occasionally. The result has been economic upheaval in the three major networks, all of which came under the ownership of corporations not primarily involved in news. "What we're seeing is a shift in priorities in the news business," said Ike Pappas, a veteran CBS correspondent who was laid off in a massive firing in early 1987. "What we had before was a tradition and an ethic and a responsibility to cover the story first and worry about the money later."[30]

Perhaps an even greater change in the news may lie ahead, with the advanced technology of cable networks and additional channels. One communications specialist has estimated that a city like Washington, D.C., given this technology in the foreseeable future, could have two hundred television and hundreds of radio stations, each presenting programming for narrow segments of the population. This means that large, general stations would go the way of general magazines like *Life*, *Look*, *Colliers*, and *The Saturday Evening Post*, which were replaced by narrow-interest publications.

In 1982, the Senate Commerce Committee conducted hearings on what legislation was needed in order to keep abreast of such developments.[31] Sen. Robert Packwood, R-Ore., then the chairman, speculated that radio stations might become like magazines, appealing very narrowly to an audience of only a few thousand. Harry E. Smith, CBS vice president for technology, predicted that as legal requirements for a specified amount of public-service programming are removed, stations would be able to survive with smaller audiences.

"Of hundreds of radio stations, you might have three or four that would try to be broad," Packwood said, adding that the others would specialize. "If you apply the same public service and content requirements to all two hundred stations, you're not getting diversity, you are getting repetition."

Old regulations of the Federal Communications Commission provided for "processing guidelines," under which a station seeking license renewal was judged by the amount of programming devoted to news and public service. The FCC's "public interest obligation" still requires programming of interest to local communities.

Smith said: "There's little value in reporting a sunny day on two hundred stations . . . Given the freedom to program, the stations will find audience interests, and I think, serve them." Smith speculated that not only news headlines but weather forecasts, constantly updated sports scores, box office ticket availability, supermarket specials, complete stock market quotations, and even a community bulletin board might be available by switching channels. This smorgasbord of information might become the real working definition of news.

Solomon J. Buschbaum, executive vice-president for Bell Telephone Laboratories, predicted that telephones and television sets will merge into a single instrument, with the customer having the capability, for instance, to dial up sections of newspapers in Chicago, Los Angeles, or another major city. "I will be able to structure my own menu of information that I receive, whenever I want," he said.

"You literally could wake up at seven o'clock in the morning, hear there's been a flood near Fresno, California, punch in 'Fresno flood' and out will come something from the *Los Angeles Times* on your screen," Packwood said.

"And you could push a button and something will come out on your set in printed form?"

"That is correct," Buschbaum replied. He added that there would not only be news, but access to scientific, literary, or racing information stored in data bases. Publication would take the form of institutional entities creating stores of information. The capability could be taken to every home and small business. Packwood asked what the ramifications of these electronic developments would be for newspapers. "I don't believe the printed word on the printed page is going to go away," Buschbaum replied.

But there are perils. As people become more particularized in the news they can select, they may, in the process, eliminate the parts of reality they do not like. Then truth will suffer. The mere profusion of information does not assure that truth—the heart of the matter—will emerge. It will be even more incumbent on the editor and the consumer of news to select the information that does drive to the heart of the matter.

PART II

# The Stories

# CHAPTER 6

# Campaigns and Candidates

## 1988: HART AND ADULTERY

On a May weekend in 1987, at the start of the long presidential campaign, Gary Hart headed for his Capitol Hill townhouse in Washington. Lee Hart, his wife of twenty-eight years, was back at their home in Colorado. Reporters from the *Miami Herald,* acting on a telephoned tip, secretly staked out the townhouse. They reported they saw Hart and a young actress-professional woman named Donna Rice enter the home Friday evening and depart Saturday night. The *Herald* bannered the story in its Sunday morning edition. A mere four days later, in the firestorm of controversy that erupted, during which a *Washington Post* reporter asked Hart point-blank whether he had ever committed adultery, Hart withdrew from the race.

Early in June 1987, the *Cleveland Plain Dealer,* quoting "several sources close to the governor," reported that Ohio Governor Richard Celeste, "who is considering a run for the presidency," had been "romantically linked" with three women. Celeste did not become a candidate for president. About that same time, the *New York Times* sent all professional candidates a questionnaire. "How should a hypothetical presidential candidate who has not committed adultery answer the question, 'Have you ever committed adultery?'" the *Times* asked. "How should a presidential candidate who has committed adultery answer the same question?" Most candidates refused to answer the questions.

Those were not the only developments in what became the "year of character." Sen. Joseph Biden had to withdraw in September when it was reported that he had lifted portions of his stump speech from British Labor Party leader Neil Kinnock and that he had plagiarized a bit as a law student. Days later, Gov. Michael Dukakis had to fire two of his top aides when it became known they had given to the *New York Times,* the *Des Moines Register* and NBC a video they had specially prepared, showing Biden and Kinnock on a split screen giving the same speech. U.S. Circuit Judge Douglas Ginsburg had to withdraw his nomination to the Supreme Court when it was revealed he had smoked marijuana as a college student and as a Harvard faculty member.

Had the press gone too far? Was the sexual behavior of Hart and Celeste the business of anybody but themselves and their wives, who defended their husbands? Was a president or a presidential candidate henceforth never to be permitted any privacy? Was the press going to go on fishing expeditions to try to hook even candidates about whom there were no rumors? As Hart said in an angry withdrawal speech, had the system "reduced the press to be hunters and presidential candidates to being hunted"?

If the *Herald* was right in secretly staking out Hart's townhouse (but sloppy in the way it did so by leaving the back door unattended and abandoning the stakeout during the early morning hours), was the *Plain Dealer* right in its stories about Celeste? and the *New York Times* in its blanket questionnaire? Should the press be restricted from asking certain questions? Should the *New York Times,* the *Des Moines Register* and NBC have used the stories about Biden without identifying the source?

In the "year of character," as our glimpses at Hart, Biden and Dukakis demonstrate, the role of the press in probing character is not clear. E. J. Dionne Jr., chief political correspondent of the *New York Times,* and Marvin Kalb, director of Harvard's Barone Center for Press, Politics and Public Policy and former NBC chief diplomatic correspondent, both defended the *Miami Herald*'s right to cover Hart's nighttime activities but both said they were not very comfortable about the story at all.[1]

## Guidelines

It is impossible to draw fixed rules for such stories. Every story must be judged on its own merits. But here are some tentative approaches.

*1. Who (appropriate subjects)*    Guideline: The people, and hence, the media, are entitled to scrutinize their leaders' lives to the extent that those leaders are perceived as representing them and speaking for them. Such leaders would generally be elected officials, although other high officers, such as Supreme Court justices, would also be included.

Reporters must apply a principle of "hierarchy." This guideline clearly applies to the President of the United States and candidates for that office. The *Miami Herald* met this guideline; the *Plain Dealer* did not, since Celeste was not a candidate and the allegations were not current. This guideline also applies, in a gradually lessening degree, to other elected executives, such as governors and mayors. It also applies to members of Congress, state legislatures, city councils and county commissions. Obviously, the head of the urban mass transit program and the city street commissioner and the water works superintendent were hired for their skill and expertise, and they have a right to be judged only on that basis. A lower official in a regulatory commission during the Reagan administration was accused of abusing his wife. The *Wall Street Journal's* coverage of this incident, again, was proper. Even though the official was not a "leader," he allegedly had done something illegal. Illegal acts are not protected by the right to privacy.

How about the private behavior of a member of the Cabinet? or an ambassador? This will vary. The ambassador who is sleeping with an official in a client country with which the United States has sensitive relations surely must come under scrutiny.

In a perverse sort of way, whom and what the public gossips about is a clue to the amount of trust invested in an official. Gossip occurs only when there is intense personal interest. The public gossips about the president and his family. The public does not gossip about whether the U.S. trade negotiator or the head of the U.S. Postal Service is involved in an affair.

Thus, the job itself and the public it serves define how much scrutiny of it there ought to be, not the press. But persons outside the candidate's family surely ought to be exempt from such scrutiny. It is no accident that presidential brothers, who have had little or nothing to do with the policies of the president, have suffered from the glare of public attention.

*2. What and Why (relevance)*    Guideline: We are multidimensional but integrated persons. It is impossible to isolate part of our existence from the rest of it. There is a relationship between private morality and public morality. Therefore, it is appropriate for the press to probe private morality.

A few years ago, I had a breakfast conversation with a man who was a national politician's campaign chairman in a major state. The chairman was upset. He said he had had difficulty even getting a telephone call through to the politician's chief aide. With some anger, the chairman speculated to me that the aide's rather bawdy public behavior was directly related to the cavalier way in which the aide had responded to him. He went on to draw a more general analogy between public and private behavior.

"I'm a liberal," the chairman continued. "I used to say that all I care about is how a senator votes on a particular issue; that I don't care what the senator does in his private life. I don't say that any more. There is a relationship."

At Drew University's 1977 Conference on Private and Public Ethics: Tension between Personal Integrity and Institutional Responsibility in American Life, David Little, an ethicist at the University of Virginia, said: "It's impossible to divide public from private morality in any neat, dichotomous way. Any simplistic division or notion of two moralities will not wash." Little's contention was echoed by virtually every other participant.

If the candidate's private life is in disarray, what does this suggest about his public life? Has the candidate portrayed himself as different from the way he actually is behaving?

"Behavior which goes to the question of candor, character, judgment, self-discipline, and personal responsibility in a presidential campaign clearly falls within the category of information that citizens need to exercise their intelligent responsibilities as citizens of a free country," said David Broder of the *Washington Post*, perhaps the nation's leading political reporter.[2]

Gary Hart had been the subject of rumors about "womanizing" ever since he was the youthful national campaign manager for George McGovern's 1972 presidential campaign. As Hart's own presidential ambitions began to flourish, other facts became known—he had changed his name from Hartpence, he had changed the style of his signature, and perhaps most significant, he had tried to downplay his Church of the Nazarene background. He knew—and knew very well, indeed—the beliefs and behavior of a Fundamentalist Christian. Hart was not a person who had gone to a Fundamentalist Sunday School as a boy and then had fled forever. He was a graduate of Bethany Nazarene College, and his wife, Lee, and her sister, Martha Keys, who became a congresswoman from Kansas, were daughters of one of six general superintendents of the Church of the Nazarene. All this, plus Hart's "loner" reputation in the U.S. Senate, suggested a person not at peace with his roots.

It must be acknowledged that adultery may be one basis on which to vote for or against a candidate, but it is *not* the only one or even necessarily the most important one. Thus, voters should not necessarily have cast ballots for Thomas E. Dewey over Franklin D. Roosevelt in 1944 or for Richard Nixon instead of John F. Kennedy in 1960 merely because of allegations that Roosevelt and Kennedy had affairs. (It should be pointed out that these allegations were not publicized at the time.)

Hart's behavior with Ms. Rice did not involve merely the allegation of adultery. That allegation, coupled with Hart's change of his name and age, his unease with his early beliefs, led to serious questions about his character. Whether a person sees adultery as permissible or morally wrong (in the same news conference Hart replied to another question that he believed adultery to be wrong), adultery suggests an attitude that sees women as sex objects.

The secret affair suggests deceitful and duplicitous behavior that raises the question of whether the candidate as president also would engage in deceit and duplicity in his official acts. On the other hand, to confess adultery to a spouse may indicate blatant insensitivity on the part of the one making the confession—the partner making the confession may experience a catharsis, but while doing so, shifts the burden for dealing with the adultery onto the other spouse, who may already be so emotionally battered in the relationship as to be unable to handle the dreaded new information. Obviously, a couple in which one spouse has committed adultery must deal with this privately in some way if they wish to keep the marriage together. Confession one to the other, although painful to both, may be a step in the healing process. But the situation gets infinitely more complicated if the couple is well known. Hart's public acknowledgment surely was a humiliation to his wife. Clearly, one way to avoid this Hobson's choice is not to commit adultery.

Hart's willingness, even eagerness, to engage in questionable public behavior may have indicated a "deathwish" for his candidacy. In an interview in the *New York Times* published the same day as the first *Miami Herald* story, Hart had invited the press to shadow him. But adultery is not necessarily an all-revealing character trait. After all, Oliver North acknowledged during the 1987 Senate Iran-Contra hearings that his fidelity to his wife had not prevented him from lying in the course of his official duties on the National Security Council staff.

We cannot dismiss allegations of adultery as irrelevant or merely incidental. These allegations can make up part of the data bank by which a citizen can decide how to vote—and each citizen can decide for himself or herself how much importance to attach to those allegations. The citizen decides on the basis of as much information as possible; it is not the political reporter's or editor's role to act as de facto censor.

3. *How (probable cause)*    The best way to check a candidate's character is to observe him or her over an extended period of time. How does the candidate relate, especially in unguarded moments, to equals? to underlings? to his wife? What is the candidate's temperament like? Is

he tense? volatile? Jimmy Carter burst to fame in the early 1976 primaries partly on the strength of the warmth of his smile. But reporters who covered him over an extended period came to sense that behind that smile was a certain feeling of being ill at ease in political situations. This conclusion was heightened by the observation that he seemed much more natural and at ease when attending his Sunday School class or speaking to a black audience, two groups with which he had been intimately involved since his early years. These clues pointed later to glaring defects in Carter's ability to deal effectively with Washington politicians.

Such observation requires acute perception. It involves constant checking and rechecking of any conclusions one might draw about the candidate. Reporters, after all, are not psychologists.

If there appears probable cause to suspect that something about the candidate is awry, then reporters may have to take another step, such as an investigation which in its most extreme form may become a stakeout at a private residence. The rumors about Hart and a specific tip gave the *Miami Herald* the right to proceed with a stakeout. But surely the *New York Times* questionnaire lacked that probable cause. Stakeouts are clearly a less desirable way of checking a person's character. Stakeouts of public officials and public events have been going on as long as there has been a press corps. I once estimated that twenty percent of my time covering the White House was spent on stakeouts—on weekends at the Cozy Inn while President Carter was nearby at Camp David, or outside the White House waiting for presidential visitors to leave so we could buttonhole them. What made the stakeout of Hart's townhouse different was that it was done in secret. The secrecy made it an embarrassing, even sleazy technique.

In some ways, the press showed remarkable restraint in writing about Hart's behavior, of which it had been aware for fifteen years. It was as if the press had been saying—both to Hart and the public—"Look! We don't really care about signatures and birth dates and sexual mis- demeanors. But we have reason to believe there is a pattern in Hart's behavior and character that is repugnant to many Americans. Read our lips! Read between the lines of what we are saying."

*4. Basis*    What is the basis for pursuing such a story? Is the tip based on something substantial? Can the tip be independently verified, as the *Herald* did in checking out Donna Rice's airline flight from Miami to Washington? If these questions can be answered satisfactorily, pro- ceed. But a fishing expedition, such as that conducted by the *New York*

*Times,* smacks of laziness at best and a witch-hunt at worst. It clearly was wrong, and the candidates were right to refuse to respond to it.

What about charges made by the opposition camp on a "background" basis in which the source does not need to be identified, or, as in the case of Senator Biden, where the Dukakis camp acted as a conduit for the charges?

When one candidate makes a charge, or relays a charge, about another candidate for the same office, the media have an obligation to identify the source of the story. The candidate making the charge has something to gain at the expense of the target of the charge. Under these circumstances, the cloak of anonymity ought not provide protection for the source.

This protection should be extended, however, to "whistleblowers" who have no personal stake in what they are disclosing and who may be acting solely for the public good. Middle-level bureaucrats who have nothing to gain personally by exposing corruption or malfeasance by their superiors need anonymity to protect against dismissal or being assigned to hollow jobs with no responsibility.

*5. Fairness*    Has the accused been given ample opportunity to respond? The *Miami Herald* confronted Hart face to face, although it dashed into print with a story that might have been held a day so that some of the holes could be filled in. Are the acts in question recent and ongoing—as in the case of Hart—or did they take place years ago? Celeste's alleged adultery took place years earlier. Pat Robertson's first child was born a few weeks after Robertson's marriage thirty-three years earlier. The *Wall Street Journal,* which disclosed this evidence of Robertson's premarital sex, treated it in appropriate fashion in the middle of a long story. Other media, which picked up the story, treated it with glaring headlines. People have the right to make amends and change.

## COVERING CAMPAIGNS

*Form*

During the course of three presidential campaigns that I covered, three serious problems arose: (1) a greater focus on the process of the campaigns than on the issues and candidates, (2) the emerging dominance of television as a campaign tool, and (3) pack journalism.

*1. Process.*    Political reporters and sports reporters are alike in that they cover the *process* more thoroughly than other reporters on their beats. There often is excessive emphasis on process at the expense of analyzing the issues and defining the candidates.

What is the candidate's southern strategy? Who is the candidate's campaign manager? press secretary? pollster? What elected officials are endorsing the candidate? The amount of detail about the campaign that gets into print is staggering—and, I fear, often irrelevant.

Critics of campaign coverage often point to the huge amount of time and space devoted to the early Iowa caucuses and New Hampshire primary compared with the later big-state primaries.[3] These criticisms, however, overlook the fact that in an era of mass communications, coverage of the Iowa caucuses and New Hampshire primary does as much to inform the voters throughout the nation as it does to inform the voters in those two states. The mass media make this possible.

*2. Television.*    What each candidate does in the "retail" campaigning in a relatively small state like Iowa or New Hampshire is quickly beamed nationwide. More significantly, though, as the campaign moves to the larger, industrialized states and the South's "Super Tuesday" primary, the candidates are forced to rely increasingly on television to get their message beyond the living rooms to the masses. And when the general campaign arrives, the candidate builds his campaign around touching down at three big media centers each day, timed so that the visits can make the evening or late night news shows.[4]

For a president seeking reelection, it is called "Rose Garden" campaigning. Every modern president has engaged in it. The president can campaign through carefully staged events without leaving the White House. As president, he can be assured of televised coverage. And by timing his arrival and departure, he can guard against all but a shouted question by a reporter.

But often television coverage fails to communicate the essence of the candidate. In 1976, the networks had wrap-ups at 11:30 P.M. on that Tuesday's primaries. Inevitably, the story was: Will Jimmy Carter's win in the Iowa caucuses give him an added push for the New Hampshire primary? And a couple of weeks later, will Carter's New Hampshire showing affect his performance in his native South? By the time the Democratic convention rolled around in Madison Square Garden and Carter was nominated, many people still said, "Jimmy who?" As I point out later, our coverage of Carter at home in Georgia that summer did little to illuminate clearly and accurately who he was.

This has made candidates very dependent on being personally

skilled in the use of television and on having a campaign that is built around TV. But one's ability to *act* a role is different from one's ability to *be* that role. Television promotes "merchandising" at the expense of genuineness.

During the 1988 presidential primaries, on the January 25 evening news, CBS anchorman Dan Rather and Vice President George Bush got into a near shouting match on live television. Rather kept pressing Bush on his part in the Iran-Contra affair; Bush responded by asking Rather how he would like it if he were judged exclusively by the six minutes in which he had walked off the "CBS News" set in protest of coverage of a prolonged tennis match.

It seems to me that both men did what they felt was expedient for them to do—acted out a sort of all's fair in love and war attitude. Rather questioned aggressively, as is his right, and Bush came back with a sharp, if personal, retort. To me, it demonstrated one of the key issues that television has not resolved in its young life: that television often thrusts the TV reporter into the story where the reporter does not belong. Had a print reporter conducted this interview, the harsh dialogue would have been edited out. I interviewed George McGovern after the 1972 election while he was winding down in the Virgin Islands. I asked him some question—I don't remember what it was, if he would run again, or if something had played a factor in his defeat. He swore and threatened to end the interview. Of course, I did not put that in my story (perhaps I should have).

3. *Pack Journalism.*    The same political reporters tend to cover the same campaigns. They are good friends, they stay in the same hotels, they eat meals together, they cover the same events, and most important, they talk with each other. Their stories often are more noteworthy for their similarities than for their differences. One reporter's fresh idea is soon recycled by the others. Worse, pack journalism guarantees that erroneous perceptions are almost written in stone.

For instance, after the 1972 Democratic convention, McGovern was viewed as weak and indecisive as a result of his initial "one thousand percent" support in the Black Hills for his running mate, Sen. Thomas Eagleton, followed by his dumping of Eagleton a few days later. That perception fed stories for the rest of the campaign. When Lyndon B. Johnson and Gerald Ford became president, they were portrayed as men from Texas and Michigan; actually, both had been living in Washington for nearly thirty years. When Ford became president, he stumbled and hit someone on the head with a golf ball, and he was caricatured as a klutz for the rest of his administration. In fact, the former

Michigan Wolverine football center was the most accomplished athlete of any recent president.

When a perception is flawed or erroneous, it is self-perpetuating and future stories tend to build on it. The result can be gross distortion.

Pack journalism is useful in that it helps protect the lone correspondent who must keep abreast of everything that is going on in a complex campaign, and it allows for the ferment of ideas that often takes place more easily in bull sessions than for the lone operator. But on balance, pack journalism often is a barrier to truth.

There needs to be more independent thought, more independent reporting, more careful examination of the candidates themselves, if truth is to be served.

## Content

In addition to matters of character, there are other things that voters have a right to know about in a campaign:

1. *Issues.*    What are the candidates' positions on the major issues of the day? Generally, despite a popular perception to the contrary, most of the media do a good job in discussing where the candidates stand—perhaps too good a job, in fact. For often a candidate will change his position dramatically after being elected, as Lyndon B. Johnson did on the Vietnam war after the 1964 election and Vice President George Bush did in supporting Ronald Reagan's economic policies after describing them as "voodoo" during the 1980 primaries. People—especially, candidates—change their minds.

In 1984, I covered another national election—in Israel. Under its parliamentary system of proportional representation, Israelis vote for the party, not the next prime minister, although it was then common knowledge that the next head of government would be either Shimon Peres of the centrist Labor Party or Yitzhak Shamir of the rightist Likud bloc. The campaign focused almost exclusively on the issues—the three-year Israeli occupation of southern Lebanon and inflation of four hundred percent a year. I recall no campaign appearances by Peres and Shamir with their wives or families. The parliamentary system assures that the campaign is focused much more directly on issues than it is in the highly personalized American campaigns.

2. *Record.*    What is the record of the candidate in public life? Here again, the media generally attach importance to his or her record, often too much importance, for in the American system, one's public

record is less important than elsewhere. Ronald Reagan's record in public life was far less broad than George Bush's in 1980 when Reagan defeated him for the GOP nomination, as was Jimmy Carter's compared to those of the others in a crowded field in 1976.

In Israel, the public records of Shimon Peres and Yitzhak Shamir were well known. They had worked their way up through a series of party and government posts to leadership of their parties. Peres had been defense minister and opposition leader. Shamir had been speaker of the Knesset and the incumbent foreign minister and prime minister (serving both posts simultaneously). It would be impossible in Israel for someone like Ronald Reagan or Jimmy Carter, whose highest previous service was as a governor of a state, to be elected head of government. Of the recent American presidents, only Lyndon B. Johnson and Gerald R. Ford would have been at the top of their party's tickets in Israel (although, ironically, each became president after having been vice president, not because he had been a congressional leader).

*3. Campaign.*    Few things in public life are covered as minutely and carefully as presidential campaigns and professional sports. Until 1976, the wire services did not assign political reporters full time to a campaign until the nominating conventions, depending instead on local staffers to provide coverage. Nowadays, national political reporters work full time all year every year on presidential campaigns. The reporters make as many trips into Iowa and New Hampshire as do the candidates themselves—many months before the first caucus or primary. I return to this more fully in a moment.

*4. Vision.*    The key quality of a leader is to possess a dream and to be able to inspire or marshal the people to support that dream. Managerial skills are much less significant. Martin Luther King, Jr. is remembered for his dream and ability to move people. Few people know whether Abraham Lincoln and Franklin D. Roosevelt were good managers—but they were good leaders.

In 1971, I asked Wilbur Mills, who was considering a run for the presidency, what he dreamed about for America. Mills, the chairman of the House Ways and Means Committee, certainly had a public record and a command of the issues to qualify him for the presidency. "I could talk about that all night," he retorted to me. But he did not answer. The fact was that he did not have a dream and his presidential aspirations went nowhere.

*5. Essence.*    In early 1976, when Grant Dillman, the UPI vice president, assigned me to cover Jimmy Carter, he told me, "This man may become president of the United States. We must define him to the American people." That was the extent of Dillman's instructions. We both understood without saying it that I would cover Carter's campaign, his position on the issues and his public record as a governor and local official. What made Dillman's instructions distinctive was that, in effect, he was asking me to discover the uniqueness of Carter that set him apart from the other candidates.

Essence is somewhat related to character and vision but is broader than either or both of them. I discuss this below in two snapshots from the 1976 Carter and 1972 McGovern campaigns.

## 1976: CARTER, THE RURAL SOUTHERNER

In the summer of 1976, scores of journalists poured into Plains, Georgia, to cover the Democratic presidential candidate, Jimmy Carter. He had burst onto the national political scene earlier that year as a virtual unknown, and he came from a part of the country , the rural South, that was almost foreign territory to many journalists. On the eve of the fall campaign, we had come to find out about him and his roots.

But most journalists did not capture the essence of either Carter or the rural South. We wrote and spoke thousands of words about softball games played on a diamond near the high school Carter had attended, and about how competitive he was in pitching those contests. We wrote and spoke a great deal about how the hordes of tourists had changed the quiet, lazy town of Plains so that it would never be the same. The truth about Jimmy Carter, however, was far more complicated than the stories suggested, and the even greater truth was that little had changed in Plains. The economic, social, and political structure of the town remained intact, and so did the attitudes. The split in the Plains Baptist Church over integration, resurfacing even in the euphoria after Carter was inaugurated, demonstrated that. There were still separate societies, black and white. There were no black elected officials in Sumter County, and in Plains the whites controlled the money. There were separate hangouts: the articulate Charles Hicks' Starlite Club for blacks and the ebullient Billy Carter's filling station for the "good ol' boys."

I sought to counter the softball and tourist stories by putting Jimmy Carter in perspective. One article began:

> Plains, Ga.—The town of Plains is in the west end of Sumter County, a
> part of the "black belt," that arc of rural south counties stretching across

Georgia, Alabama, and Mississippi, in which the population is more than fifty percent black. In the east end of the county is Andersonville, the Civil War prison where more than 12,000 Union soldiers are buried. The scars have taken a long time to heal.

The summer of 1962 was long and hot in South Georgia. Martin Luther King Jr. was jailed in Albany, 40 miles from Plains. There was a Ku Klux Klan rally. Freedom riders were fired upon. In late August and early September four black churches were burned down only a few miles south of Plains. On Oct. 1, 1962, almost literally in the ashes of those churches and the sound of those gunshots, Jimmy Carter announced for the state legislature, his first elective office ... [5]

In the remainder of the article I traced the racial history of Carter and Plains, which came to a head, finally, when Plains Baptist Church split after he became president.

I also read C. Vann Woodward's biography of Tom Watson, the Georgia populist who was Carter's hero, and wrote a fifteen hundred-word story about him. Another dispatch dealt with the vast Carter holdings, which were worth far more than Carter had been acknowledging and demonstrated that he was a millionaire.

There was also a spate of stories during Jimmy Carter's 1976 campaign about his "born again" experience. Some of these stories, by John Hart of NBC, Bill Moyers of PBS, and Robert Scheer of *Playboy*, were noteworthy. But many, even some by network broadcasters, were superficial and often missed the point. One anchorman asked Carter whether this experience meant that he had a direct pipeline to God. When Carter first discussed his faith during the North Carolina primary campaign that March, one network, on its evening news, showed a clip of Carter speaking and then the anchorman said, "By the way, we've checked this out. This is not a bizarre, mountaintop experience. It's an experience common to many millions of Americans—particularly if you're Baptist." The anchorman should be lauded for his attempt to add depth to the story, but his comments revealed an abysmal lack of insight into religion.

# 1972: McGovern the Moralist

In one twelve-year stretch, from 1972 to 1984, the three leading Democratic presidential candidates all came from similar Fundamentalist backgrounds. For years, evangelical and Fundamentalist Christianity has provided the manpower reservoir for liberal politics. Gary Hart was an example of a man who never made peace with these roots.

Jimmy Carter is an example of a man who never abandoned his roots. George McGovern is an example of a man who left his roots but accommodated them to his world view. These roots may have been the key to understanding each of these men.

Political reporters, by and large, failed to analyze carefully the critical implications of this relationship in either Hart, Carter, or McGovern. To that extent, the press failed to discover the truth about each man and thus the public was not served.

I had covered George McGovern from his earliest days as a professional politician. It was 1956, and McGovern had resigned as debate coach at Dakota Wesleyan University to become executive secretary of the South Dakota Democratic party, a fancy title for a lowly position in that rock-ribbed Republican state. Soon he challenged Rep. Harold Lovre, R-SD, for the East River house seat. Almost daily, McGovern came to the rickety old Syndicate Building, climbed the four flights of stairs to the UP bureau (the elevator didn't start running until 8 A. M.), and hand-delivered to me a press release he personally had typed. Then he went back downstairs, and drove off to a sales barn, auction house, or the main store in town to shake hands and talk with people. He was a South Dakotan who knew South Dakotans. He was clean-cut, and to me, there was a charismatic air about him. When the votes were counted, McGovern had defeated Lovre. Sixteen years later he ran for president, and I covered him again.

Most political journalists viewed George McGovern merely as a politician with far-left ideas built on opposition to the war in Vietnam, but we did not properly define him or his basic beliefs. We did not listen carefully when he quoted Moses and Isaiah—as he did regularly on the stump—sounding like his Wesleyan preacher father in calling America to return to its old values. McGovern spelled out his moral premises in what a key aide called the most significant and interpretive speech of his campaign, at Wheaton College in Illinois. After the chapel address, one political editor remarked to me outside Edman Chapel, "I think I'll skip that." That night, the network coverage focused on McGovern's soonforgotten meeting with some union leaders in Chicago. Nothing was said about Wheaton.

McGovern's campaign, ultimately, was a moral plea for a return to ancient values. He frequently quoted Moses' words that the nation must choose between "blessing and cursing, life and death." What was continually communicated to the nation was the slogan, "1000 percent and $1,000 a year," referring, respectively, to his voiced support for Sen. Thomas Eagleton, his running mate who left the ticket after disclosure of psychiatric problems, and his welfare reform proposal.

Michael McIntyre, who coordinated religious activities for the McGovern campaign, wrote:

> Many in the working press were unable to deal with the moral categories being used by candidate McGovern. Time after time he lapsed into the language of morality, judgment and justice, only to see reporters close their notebooks, glance at each other in embarrassment or grin indulgently or look at their watches. It was as though all the refugees from countless Sunday Schools had suddenly been trapped back in a lesson from Chronicles and were waiting for the bell . . .
>
> I think what is significant about McGovern's "moralizing" is that he uses the language which is understood in Midwest and southern Bible belts—and he used it without manipulation and cynicism. It is as valid an indigenous language as any we possess in this country, and his stewardship of it always reveals his own systematic grasp of its nuances. Unlike President Nixon, McGovern uses that language as his own. At Wheaton it was authentic and it said precisely what it meant—if you could understand the nuances. My judgment is, again, that many in the working press could not; and in that respect, we had an uninterpreted campaign.[6]

Because Nixon campaigned from the Rose Garden that fall and the Watergate scandal had not yet been fully uncovered, the American people cast their ballots in 1972 with incomplete knowledge about *both* Nixon and McGovern. The press must carry a huge responsibility for this.

CHAPTER 7

# The White House

*(The comments in this chapter apply as well, in varying degrees, to governors and mayors.)*


## THE PRESIDENT


The White House press corps covers the president as thoroughly as any person in the world is scrutinized, more thoroughly than political reporters cover the candidates. In fact, there is almost no comparison. The president is many things—chief executive, commander-in-chief, head of state, head of government, and perhaps most important, symbolic leader of the nation, the "father figure," so to speak, of the American people. The aim of the exhaustive coverage of the president is not merely to capture his every words on policy matters or to determine how his health is that day; in large part, it is to help paint a multidimensional portrait of this "leader of the people." Thus, the White House coverage is entirely appropriate.

A fortnight before Carter left office, in January 1981, he made a trip to Plains to set up his mother's house as his office. Many of the veteran Carter watchers made that last trip, although the eyes of most Washington reporters were on the incoming Reagan team. A few of us decided to invite Carter and his wife to Le Normandie, the country French restaurant that was one of the very few new establishments that survived around Plains after his presidency was over. The dinner, by prearrangement, was off the record, meaning nothing could be written about it at the time. Ralph Harris of Reuters and I were cohosts. Others at Carter's table included Curtis Wilkie of the *Boston Globe*, Ed Walsh of the

*Washington Post,* Sam Donaldson of ABC, and Al Sullivan of Voice of America. I pondered whether to let the conversation drift in a pleasant, nonserious direction, or to try to direct it toward more serious matters. There would never be another opportunity like this. So midway through the meal, I asked Carter to assess foreign leaders he had met. It triggered a significant and revealing conversation.

The first full account of the dinner was made twenty-two months later when Curtis Wilkie of the *Boston Globe* contrasted what Carter had said off the record with what he had written in his newly published memoirs, *Keeping Faith.* Thus, I am now free to write about the dinner.

Carter agreed with me that former Senegal President Leopold Senghor, an eminent French philosopher, came the closest of any leader he had met to Plato's ideal of the philosopher-king. Egyptian President Anwar Sadat was his favorite. He said Soviet President Leonid Brezhnev was "a man of peace" who didn't want war, but added, "I don't mean he's a Quaker." Israeli Prime Minister Menachem Begin was the most "difficult" leader he had dealt with. At this point, Carter quipped that the only two things he wanted to leave to Ronald Reagan were Menachem Begin and Sam Donaldson. Donaldson, at the table, loved it, of course, and the quip not so mysteriously made its way into print within days.

Carter said French President Valery Giscard d'Estaing had immense power under French law, was strong and practical, and the Western leader with whom he had the closest relationship. He expressed special admiration and affection for former Canadian Prime Minister Joe Clark, the late Japanese Prime Minister Nasayoshi Ohira, and the late Yugoslav President Josip Tito. Carter said West German Chancellor Helmut Schmidt would "stab you in the back." He said he liked former British Prime Minister James Callaghan, and sometimes wears a suit made of material given him by Callaghan with the pin stripe formed of the letters, "JC."

At home, Carter said, former Secretary of State Henry A. Kissinger was "brilliant but devious." Deputy Secretary of State Warren Christopher, then in the final stages of negotiations resolving the Iran hostage crisis, was the most competent public servant in his administration, and White House domestic affairs adviser Stuart Eisenstadt was next. Carter said he chose Sen. Edmund S. Muskie, D-Maine, instead of Christopher to succeed Secretary of State Cyrus Vance because he wanted someone with a reputation. He praised Rep. Jack Brooks, D-Tex., chairman of the House Government Operations Committee, as a "tough son-of-a-bitch" and anyone's best ally on Capitol Hill.

And he said the State Department's "inertia" often kept it from producing original ideas. He said it was filled with careerists who were so expert in or devoted to single nations or regions that it became impossible to get broad advice.

It was a riveting discussion.

## Saturation Coverage

While he was president, I wrote occasional dispatches on Carter the outdoorsman, Carter the lover of culture (who attended the Kennedy Center about thirty times, compared to a grand total of three for Ford and Nixon), and especially, Carter the born-again Christian. No single story in itself defined him, but all of them together provided a multidimensional look at Carter and helped to explain his actions as president.

I estimate I heard ninety percent of all the words that Jimmy Carter spoke in public as president, a number greatly enhanced by my trying to attend Sunday School the fifteen or twenty times he taught his class while he was in office.

I felt it especially important to do this, for Carter's Christian beliefs were the key to understanding what motivated him. As president, Carter continued his practice of teaching Sunday School frequently. Almost from the start, the only reporters to cover those classes were the White House "pool," made up of correspondents from the two wire services and one network. On one typical occasion, the network reporter noted in his pool report, which is distributed to all other White House reporters, that Carter taught and "nothing else of substance occurred during Sunday School." Even if a journalist has no interest whatsoever in faith and religion, he or she ought to be concerned about how those factors affect a president.

The big flaw in press coverage of Carter's faith was not in misunderstanding his "born-again" experience (although that was serious enough) but in failing to see the ramifications of that experience in shaping major decisions of his presidency. As a matter of fact, my own systematic handling of Carter's faith[1] uncovered a great deal about the way he viewed the world and his own responsibilities. One area, that of power, proved to be highly significant in his presidency.

Early in his term of office, Carter remarked to employees at the old Department of Health, Education and Welfare that he came to them not as "First Boss" but "First Servant."[2] About that same time, he remarked to the elite religious and political audience at the National Prayer Breakfast: "When the disciples struggled among themselves for superiority in God's eyes, Jesus said (paraphrasing Matt 20:27), 'Whoever would be chief among you, let him be his servant.' Although we use the phrase—

sometimes glibly—'public servant,' it's hard for us to translate the concept of a president of the United States into genuine servant."[3]

Carter saw power mainly to be used as servanthood and rarely as force, and indeed, he was the first American president in fifty years not to send American troops into combat. His concept of power suggested that he would use force with restraint and moderation, an interpretation confirmed by one of Carter's key aides. In my view, this explained Carter's restraint and caution in dealing with the Iranian hostage situation and the 1979 Soviet invasion of Afghanistan. During his final campaign, he frequently remarked: "I have always tried to use America's strength with great caution and care and tolerance and thoughtfulness and prayer," and "Once we inject our military forces into combat, as happened in Vietnam, it's hard to control it from then on, because your country loses prestige if you don't ultimately go ahead and win."

I tried to trace the link between Carter's immersion in the Bible and his interest in the Middle East and human rights, a connection he himself acknowledged.[4] When I suggested in a January 1981 analysis of his presidency that the root of these views lay in Carter's understanding of Scripture, Carter remarked, "I read your series, too. That's pretty accurate."[5]

It is the sum total of these various functions that makes the reporter vitally interested in every aspect of the president's life. In short, I firmly believe that the media's questioning and examination of the president at every reasonable opportunity is nothing less than a moral imperative.

Until Richard Nixon became president, the White House reporters met in the vestibule of the West Wing, where they could easily observe those coming and going. Nixon covered over the swimming pool between the White House proper and the West Wing and converted it into a much larger press room. Now, the press room is constantly jammed with reporters. The press room is no place for the claustrophobic because reporters spend all their time either in the briefing room or in their tiny cubicles—for, aside from the press secretary's suite, access to the rest of the White House or even the Executive Office Building is not permitted without advance clearance and an escort.

Despite what appears to the public as saturation coverage of the presidency, the total amount of time measured even in *minutes* that a president is out in public and/or accessible to reporters in a week is in fact small. A comment from a White House aide or spokesman often will not do as a substitute—the president's own words are a thousand times more valuable. The White House reporter must make use of every conceivable moment of these infrequent times when the president is accessible.

The reporter seeks not only to get the president's comment but also to learn something about his personality, his character, what motivates him. Psycho-reporting is always risky, but watching the president at every opportunity day after day, week after week, can reveal much about how he relates to people, his style, even his thoughts.

## The Blurted Question

So the White House reporter has to resort to unconventional means—often criticized by the public as being rude—to get the president's comment on something. The reporter will toss a question during a ceremonial photo-taking session in the Oval Office, or shout a question over the roar of *Marine One* parked on the White House South Lawn as the president walks out to the helicopter. These questions may not always be expressed politely but they are legitimate, if not always absolutely necessary, in an informed democracy. (Should the president think the questions rude, he should be glad he is not a prime minister in Israel, England or Canada, facing daily grillings in parliament of a type that makes the White House reporters look almost wimpish.)

## The News Conference

One of the most dramatic ways for the president to make news is through use of the presidential news conference, which has varied greatly in style and form during the modern presidency. The news conference has a value that goes beyond the most obvious one of making news. After all, not all news conferences produce headlines. The news conference is a symbolic forum in which the leader stands before the people so that they may examine him, in the persons of the reporters who act as the people's surrogates.

In a real way, the news conference belongs to the reporters, not the president, even though it is the chief executive who calls a session with the press. This was illustrated on August 6, 1977 when President Jimmy Carter called a news conference back home in Plains, Georgia, to announce his welfare reform proposal, with two members of his Cabinet on hand to help explain it. Carter stated at the outset of the news conference that he wanted all questions to be about welfare reform, but a key development had just occurred in the financial affairs of Budget Director Bert Lance about which Carter had not yet commented. I was standing in for Helen Thomas, dean of the White House press corps, so I began the news conference by asking the president a question about Lance. Carter smiled, said he wished to keep the questions restricted to welfare—and answered the Lance question. Carter knew that a news conference rightfully belongs to the press, not the presidency.

To the casual layman, it may appear that the president is a lonely figure before a mob of shouting, arm-waving reporters. The reality is, however, that the president—not the reporter—has the clear advantage in the confrontation of a news conference. Most reporters take fierce pride in their independence and most would not willingly acquiesce in another person, even their editor, ordering them to ask a certain question. In nearly five years of covering the White House, I never once was told what question to ask. Other White House reporters may have been, but if so, they never admitted it. So the reporter who asks a question is asking what he or she alone has decided to ask. The president, on the other hand, has the benefit of having been prepared for the news conference by his aides, who in turn were prepared by their aides, and so on, down several levels of aides. These aides can predict with great accuracy what questions will be asked, and they can prepare the president to give the answer he wants to give. The president almost always knows far more about any imaginable topic than the reporter who asks the question. It is the reporter, not the president, who stands as David fighting Goliath.

Franklin D. Roosevelt had news conferences twice a week, but this was before the day of televised news conferences and a mammoth press corps, and his words could not be used in direct quotes. Harry S. Truman, easily the president most beloved by reporters, held 322 such sessions in five years. Dwight D. Eisenhower had 193 in his full two terms. John F. Kennedy, the first to hold live televised news conferences, had 64 in his 1,000 days. Lyndon B. Johnson had 135 in five years; Richard Nixon, who first permitted the follow-up question, had about 30. Gerald Ford, well used to dealing with reporters from his days on Capitol Hill, had 39 in two and a half years. Jimmy Carter, who promised during his campaign to hold news conferences every two weeks, kept his word initially but his total was 59 during his four years. Ronald Reagan, who had trouble with facts and expressing himself extemporaneously despite his reputation as "the Great Communicator," had only 41 news conferences during his first seven years in office. Toward the end of his administration, the question after one of Reagan's rare news conferences was not *what* Reagan had said but *how* he had said it.

## Air Force One

A "tight pool" made up of the two wire services, a network correspondent, another print reporter, wire service photographers, and a network camera crew always accompanies the president and rides in a special section in the rear of *Air Force One*. (It actually is much more fun to ride the press plane, a chartered commercial liner with first-class configuration throughout the cabin, in which the food and beverages are better and more abundant—not to mention the rowdy camaraderie.) But *Air Force One* also is critical in providing a frequent opportunity for the president, if he chooses, to chat at leisure with a small group of journalists. Presidents have frequently done so. The information and insights gained were often immeasurable.

Soon after being assigned to the White House in May 1975, I was on *Air Force One* when President Ford returned from Mackinaw Island, Michigan. Soon after we were airborne, Ford, who had been out playing golf and had stubble on his chin, came back to chat. It was during the time when he had been vetoing bill after bill. Midway through the conversation, I asked Ford how all those vetoes were affecting his old relationships on Capitol Hill. "Oh, those vetoes are just politics," he replied. "They don't have anything to do with my friendships." It was a deep insight into Ford's basic decency and sound emotional health.

## Covering the Press

Midway through Carter's term in office, Jody Powell disclosed he was thinking about not doing the daily briefing for reporters, passing it on instead to his deputy, Rex Granum. The reason, Powell said, was that it took two or three hours each day to prepare—to read daily papers, to put out calls to the various agencies and departments about which quetions might be raised in the briefing, to get answers from them, to check on any policy matters, and to assimilate all this. As it turned out, Powell continued to brief each day. The press secretary's preparation is but a microcosm of the president's preparation for a news conference, which may be one reason why the number of news conferences tends to decline the longer the president is in office.

As a matter of fact, most of the highest officials in government are spending increasing amounts of time "covering the press." Martin Linsky and a team at Harvard's Kennedy School of Government identified and queried 1,002 top "policymakers" in Washington since the Johnson administration; they queried the 957 available present and former officials, and got 483 replies.[6] Of the respondents, 52.9 percent said they spent 0-5 hours a week thinking and dealing with the press; 27.4 percent, 5-10 hours, and 15.6 percent, 10-40 hours a week. The amount of time is increasing. Current policymakers were twice as likely to spend more than ten hours a week on the press than their predecessors. More than three-fourths of them (75.2 percent) said they had tried to seek or influence news coverage; on a scale of one to five, 53.7 percent said "three," they were sometimes successful at this; 0.6 percent said "five," always successful; and 36.4 percent said "four"—meaning that 90 percent were successful in influencing press coverage. Surprisingly, perhaps, most officials said the press had a small effect on policy rather than a large one.[7]

Presidents try various techniques to get away from what they perceive to be the "Potomac fever" or Inside the Beltway" syndrome. Carter held frequent "town meetings," in which out-of-town laymen asked the questions, and sessions with out-of-town editors. A cursory examination of these questions revealed they frequently were broad-based in nature, and not as specific as the ones Washington reporters or White House regulars asked.

Presidents also vary according to their personalities as to how they relate to members of the press. John F. Kennedy had numerous friends in the press corps. Lyndon B. Johnson was so deeply involved that he would pick up the telephone and call a photographer or a wire service deskman about a particular photo or story. Carter was somewhat reserved and rational, and to my knowledge, he met socially one on one with only two reporters during his term in office. In his memoirs, the chapter on the press fell on the cutting-room floor.

## THE PRESS SECRETARY

The two main criteria of the press secretary are: (1) Does he (there never has been a female White House press secretary) know? (2) Does he tell the truth, or, to put it another way, does he lie?

### Access

Jody Powell was glib, volatile, played favorites, didn't return telephone calls, and was often late to work. Yet, he possessed one thing that helped make him the most effective of the modern White House press secretaries: he had access to the president, no question. Powell was almost like a son to Jimmy Carter. No aide was closer. When Powell spoke, you could count on it, to use an expression Carter often employed.

The press secretary must know what's going on. Short of lying, nothing destroys a press secretary's effectiveness so much as not to know what he's talking about or not to have answers that he ought to have. Some press secretaries have served as policymakers, too. Powell wrote speeches and was one of Carter's key advisers. Larry Speakes, who had been one of Nixon's Watergate spokesman, became Reagan's chief spokesman after White House Press Secretary Jim Brady was wounded in the assassination attempt. Speakes' initial access was limited, but he gradually gained more power. He acknowledged that he began using a morning briefing to help shape foreign policy by getting a jump on the midday State Department briefing.[8]

Powell also gave the lie to another myth that often surrounds the press secretary: the notion that a press secretary should have been a journalist at some point. Powell was a political science major at the Air Force Academy and went on to finish all his work on a doctorate except for a dissertation. Bill Moyers, who was Lyndon Johnson's press secretary, had studied for the ministry. In fact, the skills of a reporter and a press secretary may not be at all similar. A reporter needs to get to the heart of the matter in a neutral fashion. The press secretary needs to know the truth, but to balance the needs of his boss at the same time. There is nothing wrong in principle with this balancing act, since it is not equivalent to lying.

## Lying

On one occasion, several former White House press secretaries were gathered at the White House and each was asked whether he had ever lied to the press. Roger Tubby, of the Truman White House; George Christian, who was Lyndon B. Johnson's last press secretary; Ronald L. Ziegler, of the Nixon White House; and Jerry Ter Horst and Ron Nessen, who served under Ford, all reported they had not deliberately lied. Powell replied that he had lied once—to protect the Iranian rescue mission in 1980.

Larry Speakes, who was President Reagan's spokesman for nearly seven years and earlier, spokesman for President Nixon's Watergate defense lawyer, acknowledged in his memoirs[9] that he used made-up quotes for Reagan at least twice—once a remark that Reagan was supposed to have made to Soviet leader Mikhail Gorbachev, and the other remarks actually made by Secretary of State George Shultz. Probably most of the words that are spoken in public by important public officials were written by their speechwriters or spokesmen. So this was not Speakes' offense. For an official can read the words, and by adopting them, the official makes them his or her own. Speakes' offense was to create the quote *ex post facto*, that is, to put words in Reagan's mouth later, words that Gorbachev, had he wished to embarrass Reagan, could have denied hearing. Speakes quoted Reagan as telling Gorbachev, "There is much that divides us, but I believe the world breathes easier because we are talking here together."

Even press secretaries do not always have access to the truth. Ziegler, recalling Watergate, acknowledged at the conference that "there was a period in the history of this country where information put forth from this podium turned out to be not true." Ter Horst resigned in protest after he was given false information about Ford's possible pardoning of Nixon. He probably spoke for the other press secretaries when he said they "are as vulnerable as the information that we get from the inside, and no more and no less vulnerable."

The press secretary is under no obligation to make full disclosure at all times. But he is under an obligation not to lie. The answer—"No comment," "I can't get into that," "That's all I'm going to say about that"—is honest and one that most reporters, although frustrated, will accept. But no one will accept a lie.

## Control

Jody Powell once estimated that the press secretary is able to control the content of about eighty-five percent of the stories coming out of the White House. (Compare this with Linsky's findings, mentioned earlier in this chapter.) The press secretary is able to do this in shaping which way the news briefing will go that day by emphasizing—or avoiding—a particular issue. The press secretary also is far more accessible to the White House reporter than are other presidential aides. He and his staff are literally only a few steps away, and they and the press corps are in constant contact. Powell frequently "wandered" into the press room, asking, "Anything I can help with?" when he had a slant or a piece of information to dispense.

This isn't merely for the convenience of the press; it's for control of the news agenda as well.

# THE CORRESPONDENT

## Superficiality

*The generalist.*    The White House reporter must be a generalist, not a specialist. The reporter must be a quick study, able to grasp the implications of a new story on page one and seeking out White House reaction to it. At any given White House briefing, the same reporter may ask questions about whether the president is going to Camp David for the weekend, how the president feels about the latest Soviet statement, whether the president is going to veto a particular piece of legislation and why, how the president feels about a recent peccadillo by his brother (there is something about a president's brother, *any* president's brother . . . ).

This is one reason why White House stories seem superficial. This is not a criticism so much as a fact of life. The White House reporter gets a quick reaction from the president or writes the initial story about a new presidential initiative. There is little time to do more than simply write the basics. It is appropriately up to the specialist reporters and columnists to do the analyzing and evaluating.

*Monolithic sources.*     But perhaps an even more important reason why White House stories seem superficial is that most are based on only one source or only one point of view. As I noted, the press secretary is able to dominate about eighty-five percent of the news coming out of the White House, and this makes the press secretary an indispensable source for the White House reporter. It is difficult to penetrate the other layers of the White House, and when a reporter does talk to other aides, almost always the aide has the same point of view and opinions that the press secretary expressed. After all, both work for the same man.

## Seduction

The White House reporter must be able to live and work regularly in chaos and often in crisis. He (or she, for an increasing number of White House reporters are women) must be able to work in close, confined quarters and be persistent enough to keep trying to penetrate the ropes, the bureaucracy, the guards, the unreturned telephone calls that keep him or her from getting the story. I once estimated that twenty percent of a White House reporter's time is spent on "stakeouts," that is, *waiting* on the curved driveway outside the West Wing for key players to emerge from a meeting with the president, *waiting* outside a house in the bitter cold while the president enjoys a leisurely meal inside, or, in the case of Jimmy Carter, *waiting* for three hours on Christmas Day afternoon along a dusty road while the president fished.

But a White House assignment, like new wine, is heady. It is exciting to have the most powerful man in the world recognize you. It is prestigious to have a television camera trained on you in a news conference. It is luxurious to have buses waiting to transport you wherever you want to go, to ride in cars with mobile telephones, to be prechecked into a hotel room with your luggage delivered from the plane to your room. In a perverse sort of way, White House reporters can sometimes come to feel that the cheers and stares of the people are directed at them as well as at the president.

But one must never allow the romance of a White House assignment to obscure the reality that such an assignment is tough and the truth can be very difficult to discover. A White House assignment may not be the best reporting assignment in Washington. In many ways, it is custodial—keeping watch over the president's public statements and movements. And often it is quite literally a "death watch"—that given the history of our nation in recent years, the reporters will be on hand if *Air Force One* crashes on take off, or if a misfit attempts to assassinate the president as he "works the fence" shaking hands with people waiting to greet him.

No one would disagree, however, that it may be the most exciting custodial job in the world.

It was the high point of the Carter presidency, October 1979. The Egypt-Israel peace treaty had been signed on the north lawn of the White House that spring; one week earlier, Pope John Paul II had made a triumphant visit to the White House. Three weeks later, on November 4, a group of Shiite Moslems would seize the U.S. Embassy in Tehran, and Carter's presidency would begin a fatal decline. No one knew this that golden October Sunday.

Carter was attending Sunday School at First Baptist Church. He slipped me a note. "Wes-" it read, "Can you have lunch with us today? (12:30 p.m.)." It was signed "Jimmy." Having my priorities in order, I scribbled across the bottom, "and Becky?" So we gathered in the family quarters of the White House for Sunday dinner.

As we sat on a sofa in the grand hallway, so large that it is used as a living room, Carter said with a smile that I had had to sit through a lot of Sunday School lessons—sort of suggesting that this had earned me the right to an invitation to dinner. We talked of our books, and he told me my book, *The Spiritual Journey of Jimmy Carter,* a compilation of his religious remarks, probably represented the "purest Carter."

At least half of our time was spent on his two grandchildren—Jason, then five, and James Earl IV, then two, the only one of the five bearing that name actually to go by it. Carter nuzzled the two little boys. He carried them in a curious way, holding them horizontally across both arms instead of putting their heads on his shoulder and supporting them with his arm under their rumps. The dinner of London broil and pie made of apples from Camp David was served in the family dining room. The boys were perched on phone books. At one point, James stuck his hand in the butter dish and Jason scolded, saying "Isn't that disgusting?" James at another point tossed an onion ring on the floor. The president picked him up—the same way, horizontally—and carried him out, saying, "James will eat the rest of his meal in the kitchen."

Again, I decided to pursue serious topics. I asked about the Florida caucuses the previous day. Carter answered quickly, and predictably, and it was clear that this was not his interest of the moment. Then I said I wanted to ask him about something I had always wanted to follow up on. I asked him to elaborate on his statements about power and servanthood. I did not know how prescient that question was because I believe his view of power explained his subsequent response of moderation and restraint in Iran and Afghanistan. Carter smiled, but did not answer directly. He said he did not like pomp, that he had dropped "Hail to the Chief" early in his presidency, but so many people criticized him that he had to restore it.

I asked if Carter wanted to talk about the pope's visit. He said (after returning from the kitchen with James) that he had asked the pope in the family quarters whether he wished to speak as two statesmen or as two friends, and the pope replied as friends. Carter said he asked him how he handled all the adulation, and the pope replied that he prayed more about that than anything else.

Carter also said he agreed with just about everything the pope had said. "I'm very conservative on the abortion issue," Carter told us. "I can't imagine Jesus agreeing to abortion." Then something happened that was the only mark on otherwise total rapport between the president and the First Lady. Carter said there was something on which Rosalynn did not agree. She interrupted to say, "Jimmy, we did not have an argument, we *discussed* it." She said she disagreed with the pope on birth control. She said she had had three sons very quickly and with Jimmy often on naval duty at sea, she did not know what she would have done if another child had come quickly. "Jesus loves me, too," she said, then repeated, "Jesus loves me, too." She made an interesting point: that anti-abortion shows love for the unborn child, but birth control shows Jesus' love for the mother.

Then Carter suggested we go into the den across the grand hallway, and he played Bob Dylan's new record, "Slow Train-a-Comin'." Carter had remarked during the meal that Dylan had become a Christian and he wanted him to perform at the White House (which never occurred). As the record played, Carter nuzzled the little boys and softly sang the words to "Man Named All the Animals." And whenever they got to the part, ". . . I think I'll call him—a pig!" or ". . . I think I'll call her—a lamb!"

they laughed with glee. At 2:25, Carter said he had two speeches to write; he thanked us for coming, and we took our leave.

As I reflect on this, the Carters appeared to do little more than extend hospitality to us in the grand tradition of Sunday dinner, a tradition of the South as well as of my own upbringing. The occasion was family-oriented; the conversation largely nonpolitical. It gave me rare insight into the president at home. Yet I must also acknowledge my own vulnerability to the flattery of an invitation to Sunday dinner at the White House, an invitation made all the more precious by the fact that similar invitations were extended to few other reporters.

CHAPTER 8

# Congress

(*The following applies as well, in varying degrees, to other parliaments, state legislatures, county boards, and city councils.*)

A personal word. My favorite assignment is a legislature. The ceremonial aura, the dynamics of heated debate, the multiplicity of sources all make the legislature, whether a city council or the UN General Assembly, lively and appealing. I got hooked while covering the 1957, 1959 and 1961 sessions of the South Dakota Legislature. I saw Congress from inside and out. I came to Washington as a Congressional Fellow under sponsorship of the American Political Science Association, spending several months in the offices of Rep. Morris K. Udall, D-Ariz., and Sen. Charles H. Percy, R-Ill. Later, I became Percy's first press aide (1967-68) and still later, a reporter on Capitol Hill (1981-83). I occasionally went to the UN General Assembly while covering the White House and to the Israeli Knesset during my three years in Jerusalem. And I have visited the Canadian parliament. All were exciting—and each was different.

No one wielded the gavel with more style and savoir-faire than House Speaker Nils Boe in South Dakota. Despite the British reputation for propriety and the typical "ugly American" reputation, the U.S. Senate is a model of decorum and courtesy. It is in British and Canadian parliaments that oaths are shouted and obscene gestures flashed. But even the British parliament cannot compare with the raucous behavior of the Knesset, where fighting and name-calling take place frequently. I love them all.

For sheer drama, nothing surpassed what happened in the South Dakota Senate in January 1957. With George McGovern winning election to Congress in the previous November, the Democrats had managed to win an eighteen to seventeen margin in the thirty-five-member State Senate. But Democratic Sen. elect Leo Kabeisiman from Yankton took ill, and state law provided that the incumbent legislator would hold office until his successor was duly elected *and sworn*. The day of the opening session came, and the Democrat was ill back in Yankton. At the last minute, outgoing State Sen. Chet Stewart of Yankton, a Republican, who had stayed hidden away in an anteroom, stepped into the chambers and took the oath, thus taking away control of the Senate from the Democrats and giving it to the Republicans by an eighteen to seventeen margin.

## Accessibility and Invisibility

Every day the U.S. Senate is "in," about ten minutes before the session begins, a flock of congressional reporters go down to "dugout chatter." They walk into the Senate chambers and there, in front of the two front-center desks, they have a mini-news conference with the Republican and Democratic leaders, the greater attention being paid, of course, to the majority leader.

The questions may be routine: How long will the Senate be "in," or meet, today? When is a final vote on a particular bill expected? Or, the leaders' reaction may be sought on a breaking page one story. Or, the session may be essentially jocular. The bell rings, marking the start of the session, and the reporters are quickly hustled out. On the other side of the Capitol, the same thing is going on with the House speaker, although that meeting is held in his office.

Contrast this with accessibility to the president or a Cabinet official. This easy accessibilty is the great difference between the executive and legislative branches. Senate Republican leader Robert Dole was far more powerful than his wife Elizabeth when she was Transportation secretary, and far more accessible.

Howard Baker fine-tuned this accessibility when he was Republican leader. After the bell sounded ending Baker's briefing, his aide, Tom Griscom, went to the corridor at the rear of the chamber and elaborated—or clarified—for reporters what Baker had said.

This same accessibility prevails throughout Congress. If a reporter wants to talk to a senator, he or she simply goes to an anteroom, has a Senate aide carry a note to the senator in the chamber, and the senator usually comes out to talk within a few moments. There are huge numbers of eager, well-coiffed, well dressed congressional aides who also are more than willing to talk to a reporter. The Senate and House press galleries also are staffed by the most courteous and helpful aides to be found in government. All this makes it far easier to obtain information in the legislative branch.

There is a simple reason for the greater accessibility in the legislative branch than in the executive branch—only one member of the executive is elected, while all legislators are. Thus, members of the legislative branch and their staffs are naturally more responsive to public opinion.

Perhaps the most dramatic accessibility provided to Congress is the decision in the past decade to televise sessions, of the House at first and later of the Senate. For years there have been televised congressional hearings. More recently, cameras have been permitted in the chambers, though always trained on the speaker rather than panning the chambers to show who is or isn't present. The honest eye of the television camera has contributed on the whole to the public's grasp of the workings of Congress. It has also rewarded the skill and ability of individual members. Viewers can look into the eyes of the speaker and draw their own conclusions about what the member is saying. The fear that publicity-conscious members would hog the camera or use it for blatantly selfish purposes has not materialized.

There is a dark side to the matter of easy accessibility. It is easy invisibility. A representative from a safe district can be elected and reelected to Congress and lose himself or herself in the 435-member House, quite safe from the public eye and press coverage. Also, most congressional districts do not have a newspaper with a correspondent in Washington. So they have to depend on news releases from the mems s of Congress themselves. And often these releases are quite self-serving and flattering—and are distributed at taxpayer expense.

"It was my experience that for every Mo Udall there was at least one Wayne Hays," says Frank Eleazer, former head of the UPI House staff. "The average level of dedication and ethical conduct among our lawmakers fell somewhere in between" (personal correspondence, 2 Feb. 1988). His reference was to Rep. Morris K. Udall, D-Ariz., a highly respected House member and my own mentor while I was a Congressional Fellow, and former Rep. Wayne Hays, R-Ohio, who served under the cloud of an accusation that he had hired a secretary primarily for sexual reasons.

## Multiple Sources

The relative ease of access in Congress has the effect of providing the reporter with multiple sources, unlike the White House, where often there is only one source. In the executive branch, technically, all officials work for the president and are generally loyal to him. In the legislature, the members are not beholden to the president, only to the people in their district, and they are much franker in speaking out.

It is almost impossible to keep anything a secret on Capitol Hill. There are 100 senators, 435 House members, and thousands of aides—and if one won't talk, another will. I often used the tactic of contacting *junior* members of Congress or committees on the theory that often reporters did not pay as much attention to them as to senior members, and thus the eager junior member, when finally contacted, tended to be much more cooperative and talkative. Furthermore, everyone talked to the leadership and generally got the same line.

On the other hand, while the White House reporter is a generalist, congressional reporters often are specialists in the area of their beats. They become incredibly knowledgeable on taxation, or health care, or the budget.

On any given day, there may be as many as twenty or thirty congressional hearings. Typically, in a three-day hearing, the first day is taken up with officials, the second day with academicians and experts on the subject, and the third with witnesses drawn from the public. Congressional reporters are faced constantly with the problem of what hearing (or often, hearings) to cover on a given day. Often, the solution is to cover the first day of the hearings only, thus skipping what might have been enlightening testimony from the experts and clues to the grass-roots popularity of the issue from the "public witnesses." Reporters often pick up the witnesses' prepared statements, omitting the questioning. The result is that although the entire hearings record of the legislation may be balanced, the press coverage is not. Further, the stories often are written from a political perspective. We need to scrutinize what the lobbyists are doing; this may well be the most unreported story in Washington. We need to reveal all the forces, not merely the legislators, that shape lawmaking.

It is unfortunate that the media are unable, because of shortage of staff and of news space, to cover congressional hearings in their entirety. The hearings often are assembled with panels and agenda that befit graduate seminars in the nation's finest universities. The media thus miss an excellent opportunity to educate the public.

A further word of caution: As stated earlier, a hearing is merely one step on the way to passage of a law. I would guess that most hearings do not result in laws. So, the hearings often serve mainly to spark debate and focus the public's attention. The reporter must be careful to make this clear in the story.

The hearings are often exciting, even for the jaded reporter. I saw the late Chicago Mayor Harold Washington and the Democratic presidential hopeful Paul Simon in action as House subcommittee chairmen—long before anyone guessed they were headed for national fame. I heard Bill Cosby and Stevie Wonder and a host of other celebrities testify.

## Saturation Coverage

The question is: Despite the number of hearings and the breadth of activity on Capitol Hill, is this really where the action is?

I wonder, given the distribution of reporters in Washington, whether the media would get closer to the heart of the matter by paying less attention to Congress and more attention to the numerous departments, agencies and commissions in which faceless, anonymous bureaucrats are making decisions through regulations and rulemaking that affect the day-to-day lives of many men, women and children. Often a lone reporter will cover several agencies and departments. It is impossible, given the size and complexity of these agencies, for a lone reporter to cover—and "uncover"—what is going on in them.

Grant Dillman, who was UPI Washington vice president and news editor, came up with a "team" plan that went a long way toward arriving at a proper balance in the executive-legislative-administrative coverage, as well as providing more insightful and skilled reporting.

Formerly, the wire services made assignments based, for want of a better term, geographically. Each wire service had a Senate staff, a House staff, an agency reporter. The idea was that the reporters could establish lasting contacts in their particular turfs. Dillman changed this approach drastically and organized reporting teams. Reporters on "the national security team," for instance, covered the Pentagon and the congressional armed services committees. The "diplomatic team" covered the State Department and the congressional foreign relations committees. In other words, the reporter went to where the story was—perhaps to Capitol Hill, perhaps downtown.

Dillman made the change at the time of Watergate. The Associated Press covered the story in the old-fashioned way—the Senate staff covered the Senate Watergate hearings, the court reporter covered the special prosecutor's proceedings, the White House correspondent covered the story when it broke there. I was a UPI principal on Watergate and went wherever the story was breaking—to the District Courthouse for the various trials and proceedings, to the Supreme Court for the arguments on the White House tapes, and with the White House press corps to Jackson, Mississippi, when during the height of the cover-up, it appeared possible that President Nixon might say something about his involvement.

The rationale was sound: The occasional source that was lost because the reporter was not in the same place consistently was more than compensated for by the greater in-depth reporting that carried a proper balance of legislative and executive detail.

The White House has one point of view and essentially one spokesman. Congress, on the other hand, has many points of view and many spokesmen. The White House often can act by presidential order; Congress must go through a protracted legislative process to get things done. These things demand different abilities on the part of the White House press corps and the congressional press galleries. But each plays an integral part in communicating to the people the truth about what their government is doing.

And I ask unanimous consent, Mr. Speaker, to revise and extend my remarks.

# CHAPTER 9

# The Foreign Correspondent

The stereotype of a foreign correspondent is a reporter who wears a trench coat and whose life is marked by dashes of romance and intrigue. The picture may not fit reality, but the reality probably is better—more exciting and more fulfilling.

## THE MIDDLE EAST

I was a foreign correspondent in Israel between 1983 and 1986, for two and a half years years as manager for Israel and for the last few months as senior Middle East correspondent. I went on short assignments to Cairo, Amman, Cyprus, and Beirut during my three-year stint, and made a dozen or more trips into southern Lebanon during the final stages of the Israeli occupation. The occupation was, actually, one of the main Israeli stories during my time there. Lebanon had become Israel's Vietnam.

As President Chaim Herzog has pointed out, Israel has the third largest number of foreign correspondents in the world. It is difficult to pin down just how many there are. About twenty-five are full-time transient American foreign correspondents, that is, foreign correspondents who are in Israel for a limited period. Perhaps a half-dozen American correspondents, however, actually have taken up permanent residence in Israel. Numerous journalists, many of whom also have moved to Israel, have full-time jobs with the Israeli press but also string for American or British newspapers. As a matter of fact, there are as many British newspapers as American newspapers with full-time correspon-

dents in Israel. The French, Germans, Dutch, and Swiss also are represented in the foreign press corps.

"The interest in everything that happens in this small country has
become a kind of media obsession the world over," President Herzog
said. "This of course has its very flattering side, but on the other hand,
this obsession frequently leads to distortions and a loss of proper proportion. Every internal event—whose objective international significance is minute to nonexistent—is inflated to irrational proportions.
Events of little importance, such as stone-throwing on the Ramot road, a
small demonstration by youths in the [occupied] territories, exchanges
between various personages in the Israeli political system, have great international reverberations."[1]

Herzog's initial remarks were accurate. But his concluding remarks
suggest the truth I touched on earlier, that most politicians would prefer
to operate in a vacuum unless what they did was viewed favorably.
Some of Herzog's examples go right to the matter of justice and injustice
in Israel. Herzog went on to blame the saturation coverage on "a tremendous number of foreign correspondents" who are in Israel because it is
"the sole democracy in this region."

The problems in the Middle East, and Israel, are enormous. The en-
mity between Arabs and Jews dates back to Isaac and Ishmael (although
Jews and Arabs often lived side by side in peace until Zionism began in
earnest in 1881). Within Israel, there is the growing problem of the ultra-
orthodox Jewish community and the more secular Jews. One fascination
of being in Jerusalem, an incredibly romantic and exciting place, was observing Arabs and Jews living side by side. I found abundant opportunities to write stories and special reports dealing with issues of justice
and peace.

The Middle East, and Israel in particular, traditionally has been a
persistent front-page story. It is unusual for a major newspaper on any
given day not to carry one to three stories out of the Middle East. This is
due in part to the region's geostrategic location as the crossroads of three
continents and two major bodies of water, the Mediterranean Sea and
the Indian Ocean. It also is due to the Middle East becoming one of the
arenas in which the rivalry between the United States and the Soviet
Union is waged. But the main reason for American interest has been the
Judeo-Christian tradition. The most important shrines of Judaism and
Christianity and the third holiest site in Islam are located in the walled
half-mile-square Old City atop well-worn mountains in Jerusalem.

I found my concern for truth, especially as linked to justice and
peace, my love of "the story," and a life deeply embedded in the Judeo-
Christian tradition and Scriptures all converging in my assignment in Is-

rael. When my tenure ended, I made an incomplete list of the feature stories and special reports my staff had done. The breakdown reflected these things: the Jewish-Arab dispute, 27; Israeli foreign policy and the occupation of southern Lebanon, 26; Israeli politics, 15; the Israeli economy, 7; life in Israel, 15; and religious-archaeological stories, 23.

There were stories about the unevenness of punishment for the Jewish and Arab offender on the Occupied West Bank (an Arab boy who throws stones at an Israeli bus would get several years in prison; a Jewish settler convicted of a systematic reign of terror against Arabs on the West Bank got as little as four months to seven years); an "anatomy" of a West Bank incident, from the time Palestinians demonstrated until Israeli troops arrived; the first-person account by former Nablus Mayor Bassam Shakaa, a militant Palestinian, whose legs were blown off by a militant Jewish settler; the Palestinian nonviolent movement. Coverage of these stories did not just happen. Each was *selected* for coverage. Sensitivity to issues of justice must be developed.

## The Routine

My editor in London instructed me to "cover Israel like a state in America." This squared accurately with the great American interest in the Middle East. Things in Israel were news in the United States that would not have been news if they were to happen in Britain or France. Someone remarked that it was easier for a death in Jerusalem to make the *New York Times* than it was for a death in New York.

People in Israel are "news junkies" far more than elsewhere. They constantly monitor the hourly newscasts on state radio. These broadcasts are piped over the bus loudspeaker. Every journalist carries a small radio, often equipped with a built-in recorder so as to allow for taping the newscast to play it back later. Israel radio had English newscasts at seven A.M. and one, five, and eight P.M., and these were sine qua non for the foreign correspondent.

If we wanted to watch English television, we tuned to Jordan TV (Israel TV was all in Hebrew). Jordan's TV newscasts were unusual. Unfailingly, the lead item was about King Hussein, Queen Noor, or Crown Prince Hassan. I think even the Battle of Armageddon would be preceded by clips of Crown Prince Hassan cutting a ribbon for a new bridge! While I was on assignment in Amman on one occasion, Jordan's Prime Minister held a rare news conference. That night, after the obligatory clips of the royalty, Jordan TV began showing the news conference from the beginning with very little editing. When the half-hour broadcast was up, the tape of the news conference was halted. The next night on the evening news, the tape was resumed!

The *Jerusalem Post* is the only English newspaper in Israel, and it is required reading for the foreign correspondent. There are a half-dozen major newspapers in Hebrew: *Ha'eretz,* perhaps the most respected newspaper in Israel; *Yediot Ahronot,* with the biggest circulation; *Ma'ariv; Davar,* the Histadrut labor federation newspaper; the *Al Hamishmar,* a leftist paper; *Hatzofeh,* of the ultra-orthodox National Religious Party; and *Hadashot,* a new tabloid which already has to its credit several scoops, including the Israeli Army's beating to death of two Palestinian bus hijackers in April 1984. Many foreign correspondents hired translators to go through these papers daily.

The government, recognizing the deep friendship between Israel and the United States, is very helpful to foreign correspondents. The Government Press Office is located in Beit Agron (Hebrew for "the House of Agron") on Hillel Street, a ten-minute walk from the Old City. The GPO daily issues English translations of a half-dozen to a dozen pieces of material—summaries of news stories and editorials in the Hebrew press, statements by the prime minister and occasionally by other cabinet members as well, summaries of key documents, announcements of military actions. The GPO supplements this with frequent announcements transmitted simultaneously to the correspondents' telephones; these announcements, perhaps of an Israeli air raid on southern Lebanon, for example, or of the Israel Navy's shelling of Yasser Arafat off Tripoli, Lebanon, in late 1983, may come in the middle of the night as easily as at midday. Since the GPO is a governmental agency, like Israel Radio, these documents carry a quasi official imprimatur, a useful sourcing device for foreign correspondents.

The Israeli Foreign Ministry has a daily background briefing at 12:15 P.M., but almost always the spokesman requires that any stories be attributed to "a government official in Jerusalem." Generally, the correspondents argue about this, because there are both Israeli and Palestinian officials in Jerusalem.

The prime minister's office, ironically, is not nearly so open. Uri Savir who was spokesman for Prime Minister Shimon Peres, had biweekly press briefings. Avi Pazner, who was Prime Minister Yitzhak Shamir's spokesman, did not have regular briefings but I found him more accessible by telephone.

Of course, the best way to cover a story is to be on the scene. My staff always covered the cabinet secretary's briefing at the end of the regular Sunday cabinet meeting. We also staffed meetings of the Knesset that were taking up key matters.

Israeli is so small a country that it is possible to drive from Jerusalem to any part of the country, to Eilat on the Gulf of Aqaba or Metullah on the far Lebanese border, and return on the same day. The government sponsors frequent trips for foreign correspondents—to Bethlehem before Christmas, for example, and to new high-tech plants. I once spent two days on an Israeli Navy gunboat, most of the time bouncing up and down while anchored off Sidon, southern Lebanon.

Yet, the foreign correspondent has to be discerning. In the fourth century Church of the Nativity in Bethlehem, the Greek Orthodox and the Armenians disagree on who has jurisdiction to clean a certain piece of the wall. During one pre-Christmas tour, the government's religious affairs adviser, acting as tour guide, made a big point of emphasizing this—and sure enough, a number of the foreign correspondents in their "annual Bethlehem Christmas story" that year wrote about the dissension in the Christian community. This was accurate, yes, but certainly not reflective of the larger truth about Christmas in Bethlehem.

Often, the correspondents do pursue the clear message the government is suggesting. No matter what, I found value in every trip to the scene, for a first-hand glimpse under the most guarded conditions is still better than no look at all.

No matter how determined the journalist, often events are happening that are not being reported. During my last year in the Middle East, probably the major story was of Israel cooperating with the United States in selling arms to Iran. I did not know about it, and neither did any of the other foreign correspondents.

## ETHICAL PROBLEMS

There are ethical problems common to most foreign correspondents.

*1. Censorship*     When censorship exists, it can be the most difficult problem for a foreign correspondent to surmount.

There is censorship in Israel, but as a practice, it is limited to stories involving the military, national security, and ongoing "terrorist" activity against Israelis. So the press is especially vigorous, and Israeli reporters are as tough in reporting on their government as foreign correspondents are.

The signing of an application for credentials from the Government Press Office represented our agreement to submit stories to the military censor. This was not hard to do, because the military censor was located just down the hall from the main offices of the GPO in Beit Agron in Jerusalem. Generally, we simply hand-carried our stories to the censor if we thought that the pieces might be sensitive. But the Israelis also monitored our wires—presumably by electronic devices automatically triggered by the use of such words as "terrorist," "nuclear," or "attack"—and they quickly pulled the plug when we attempted to transmit any stories with offending material. The only reporter whose credentials actually were jerked had flouted the Israelis, flown out of the country, and filed a story on Israel's nuclear capability. Generally, offending reporters were given a verbal slap on the wrist.

When a terrorist action is under way, the Israeli censors stop publication of any story about it for the time being. In April 1984, when Palestinians commandeered an Israeli bus on the coastal highway south of Tel Aviv, the Israelis imposed censorship from the time it was hijacked about dusk until Israeli soldiers stormed the marooned vehicle in the Gaza Strip shortly before dawn.

The Israeli censors often ran into problems. Sometimes information in one way or another fell into the hands of news organizations outside Israel, and since they were not under the censor's control, they disseminated the material without hesitation. BBC in London broadcast a story about the hijacked bus while the hijacking was in progress, and UPI used that fact as a lever to get the censor to allow transmission of at least a bare-bones wire story about the subject. Israel, of course, was unable to do anything to prevent London publication of a detailed account of Israel's nuclear facility in Dimona in 1986.

As is frequently the case, censorship was also used to cover-up wrongdoing or malfeasance. In his farewell briefing, the Israeli Army's chief spokesman, who was being reassigned, volunteered that about thirty-five Israeli soldiers—one-sixth of all Israelis lost in the opening stages of the 1982 invasion of Southern Lebanon—had been killed inadvertently when Israeli planes bombed an Israeli position and when an Israeli tank fired on another Israeli tank. Even though the information had come from the chief spokesman, the censor killed the story.

There is also de facto censorship. There are few resident foreign correspondents in most Arab countries. As I have said, the mere presence of a reporter often determines what is news. Several times more people were massacred in Hama, Syria, in February 1983 than in the Palestinian refugee camps of Sabra and Shatilla in the southern suburbs of Beirut the previous September; yet, because it was almost impossible for a foreign correspondent to get to the scene, there were few stories about it in contrast to the torrent of stories about Sabra and Shatilla. It was almost impossible for American journalists to find out exactly what was going on in Saudi Arabia when Moslem rebels seized a mosque in 1979.

"A good part of the Arab world is physically off limits to most Western journalists," says Ze'ev Chafets, director of Israeli's Government Press Office under Prime Minister Menachem Begin. "At the start of 1984, no American news organization had a resident staff correspondent in Saudi Arabia, Algeria, the Sudan, Syria, or Yemen, just to name some."[2] Accessibility is much easier in Egypt and Jordan, for instance. Almost no Arab countries require prepublication censorship. The censorship takes other forms—inaccessibility, the fear of not getting a visa renewed. If they don't like you, you don't get in again.

For three years the Syrian government refused my attempts to obtain a visa, although I had visited there on a student tour in 1964. Curtis Wilkie of the *Boston Globe*, who is sympathetic to the Arab cause, told of his difficulty in getting into several Arab countries; when he finally arrived in Damascus in late 1986, he spent three weeks there without being granted one interview with a Syrian official.

Israel is not exempt from de facto censorship. Israeli editors decided to boycott coverage of Rabbi Meir Kahane, the hard-line member of the Israeli Knesset, whose views about Arabs bordered on racism of the rankest kind.

*2. Accessibility*    How much access does the foreign correspondent have to the government, the main institutions, and the people?

Accessibility was relatively easy in Israel, but not elsewhere in the Middle East. Both Curtis Wilkie and David Lamb of the *Los Angeles Times* told Arab-American audiences of the difficulty which getting visas or making official contact in the Arab world presented to them in communicating the Arab point of view.[3]

*3. Cultural Problems*    Most American foreign correspondents are white men of European descent. They have come up through the ranks with the same overemphasis on the middle-class, political orientation that most reporters have, and are consequently vulnerable to not seeing clearly the nuances and complexities of other cultures. This vulnerability is sharply increased if the foreign correspondents have had no in-depth backgrounding in the society and institutions of the country where they are being assigned.

For instance, the difference in the Jewish and Arab views of truth is a profound source of misunderstanding in the Middle East. The Israelis tend to view truth much as Westerners do, with an emphasis on accuracy. The Arabs consider truth as a legitimate means of conveying deep feeling, and hence, their stories are often highly exaggerated by Western standards. They overstate their case in an attempt to point up its seriousness. Who is to say which aspect of truth is more important— accuracy or depth of feeling? This causes great problems for foreign correspondents, however, who often are skeptical of the factual accuracy of Arab press accounts.

On the night of 5 February, 1984, the Israeli Army spokeman announced in typically terse fashion that ten Israeli soldiers had been wounded, none seriously, in an explosion as a convoy passed through the Borj al Chameli area east of Tyre in southern Lebanon. The next morning, the state-owned Beirut Radio said that twenty-five Lebanese children and students had been killed or wounded at the Jabal Amel school by Israeli helicopter gunships and troop carriers. A short time later, in a story UPI pushed onto the wire with an "urgent" slug, Beirut Radio reported that one hundred Israeli soldiers had been killed or wounded by a suicide bomber.

I dashed to the Israeli Army spokesman to get a reaction. The spokesman, Ze'ev Chafets, who was on reserve duty that day, called it "a lie." I messaged this to our Beirut bureau, but the great bulk of the stories out of Beirut treated the killing and wounding of the twenty-five Lebanese students and one hundred Israeli soldiers as fact. It was not until the next day that I was able to sort things out through an independent source, the United Nations in Lebanon. The UN spokesman, Timor Goksel, gave this chronology:

On Tuesday evening, a roadside bomb went off near Borj Al Chemali refugee camp southeast of Tyre. No one was injured, but in the confusion, a vehicle, a white Mercedes (the cars were always Mercedes, it seemed), carrying a bomb, got in the convoy between the second and third cars. It blew up and injured several soldiers. Wednesday morning, Israeli soldiers launched a search operation at nursing and vocational schools in the area, firing away as they went.

Goksel said that there were no deaths as a result of the suicide bombing of the convoy and the firing at the school, but that thirty Lebanese were hurt, and of these, eleven needed hospitalization and four were in serious condition. Contrast these figures to the Beirut Radio count of twenty-five killed or wounded, and one hundred Israeli soldiers killed or wounded.

On April 9, 1984, the Lebanese National Resistance Front reported that a sixteen-year-old suicide bomber had driven a booby-trapped car into a group of Israeli soldiers near Jezzine in southern Lebanon, causing an estimated *fifty* casualties. A few minutes later, Israeli military sources reported the same incident, saying that *two* soldiers had been killed and two slightly wounded. In this case it was clear who was being accurate, for it would be impossible to hide fifty casualties in Israel, a small country with an aggressive press corps, where everybody knows everybody else.

Such things happened frequently. I once asked our Beirut bureau chief, who is Lebanese, about exaggerated reports. He said simply: "This is the Middle East." How does the foreign correspondent handle these vastly different, even contradictory accounts of the same incident? One way is to seek out a third-person account, as in the case of Timor Goksel. But this is not always possible. Then the journalist is left little choice but to print and carefully attribute both sides.

Some Arabs are aware of the barrier this presents to better understanding by Westerners. Mubarak Awad, of Bethlehem, is the leader of the Palestinian Non-Violence Center. One of the instructions he has given to his followers is: "No exaggerating. Tell the truth. If the Israelis take ten trees, say so. Don't say 'five hundred trees.'"

4. *The Foreign Correspondents Themselves*    Often foreign correspondents have almost no previous knowledge of the history or culture of the country to which they are assigned. This is particularly true of assignments outside the West. In my own case, I had a master's degree in Old Testament and a year's study in Hebrew, which prepared me for the critical religious dimension of the Arab-Israeli problem. But I had no background in the history and culture of the region, aside from quick briefings at the Israeli and Arab embassies in Washington before my departure for the Middle East. When I finally studied Middle Eastern history under Nadav Safran, former director of the Center for Middle Eastern Studies at Harvard, I kept saying to myself, "If only I had known these things while I was in the Middle East, if only . . . "

On the other hand, foreign correspondents can suffer from "clientitis," a malady caused by covering the same story for so long that one develops excessive loyalty to it. There is a special vulnerability to this in Israel. Nearly a third of the full-time American correspondents in Israel were Jewish or were married to Jewish women, but no apparent plot resulted from this. Hebrew is a difficult language spoken mainly by Jews, and when assignments are made to Israel, the young Jewish reporter who knows Hebrew has an advantage over the non-Jew who doesn't.

"There are today many journalists who see themselves as quasi-politicians, and politicians who view their world through the prism of television, radio, and newspapers," Prime Minister Shimon Peres commented. "This is why it is so important, in my opinion, for the government to detach itself as much as possible from media considerations—

apart from defending the freedom of the press—and for the press to detach itself as much as possible from considerations of power and politics, and to serve those whom it is supposed to serve—the public."[4]

Of more immediate seriousness, in my view, there were no Palestinians on the professional staff of any Western news organization in Israel, not one. UPI sought to correct this early during my tenure, and we hired an Arab journalist. Health problems interfered, and he was unable to continue. I regretted it very much, because what UPI did may well have forced other news organizations to follow suit.

In no situation are the external and internal barriers to truth better illustrated than in the case of the foreign correspondents. They face often insurmountable barriers of censorship and inaccessibility in the country they are assigned to cover. They often face great personal risks. At the same time, their own lack of information and understanding about that land stands as another barrier to getting at the truth.

## WAR AND OCCUPATION

I had been on an archaeological excavation at Dothan on the West Bank in 1964 when it was under Jordanian control. I shall never forget my first trip as a journalist. The Israeli Army offered to provide me with an escort for my first reporting trip to the West Bank, which Israel captured in the 1967 Six-Day War and has occupied since. The young army captain, who drove, threw her submachine gun in the front of the car before we set out and we frequently encountered Israeli troops, either in convoys or at checkpoints. There were no incidents that day, but the overall impression left on me was indelible: Israel was a land at war.

Coverage of war is difficult. Foreign correspondents rarely are permitted to observe military operations and almost always have to depend on the army to get them into combat areas. Often the reporters do not speak the language of the people and have access to only those sources the army provides. Thus, foreign correspondents see only what the army wants them to see, and talk only with those persons the army wants them to. Yet, responsible foreign correspondents do not dare risk passing up such tours because they are about the only way to get any first-hand information.

The Israeli Army also prohibits journalists from observing their operations. This extends even to the Occupied West Bank. The army publishes guidelines concerning journalists in Judea and Samaria—the biblical names Israel uses for the West Bank—when it carries out an operation. One sentence, underlined for emphasis, says: "The first obligation of the media representative is to obey area commanders, even when no written closure order is presented at the time."

In March 1985, as Israeli soldiers were withdrawing from southern Lebanon, the army censor forbade publication of the timetable for dismantling its sophisticated electronic gear atop six thousand-foot Jabal Barouk, the highest mountain in southern Lebanon, even though that timing had been disclosed during an army-conducted tour for foreign correspondents.

It was impossible for foreign correspondents to get into Southern Lebanon from Israel during the Israeli occupation 1982-85 except through tours carefully organized and conducted by the Israeli Army. Often foreign correspondents in Israel would cross the border to Lebanon at Rosh Hanikra, located on soaring chalk-white cliffs overlooking the Mediterranean, then drive five miles on a pock-marked road to Nakoura, headquarters of the United Nations Interim Forces in Lebanon (UNIFIL). The UNIFIL spokesman, Timor Goksel, was an almost legendary figure and drove through the predominantly Shiite territory in southwestern Lebanon without fear. The tours he arranged for foreign correspondents were superb.

On one such trip, in February 1985, Curtis Wilkie, Ian Black of the *Guardian* and this reporter drove through the Shiite "Iron Triangle," finally arriving at the scorched village of Maaraka. We interviewed Khalil Jradi, the twenty-five-year-old guerrilla chieftain, in his barren, second-story office where a dozen aides-de-camp sat silently lining the walls. Seeming almost unaware of us, an ethereal expression on his face, Jradi spoke in a soft voice for a half-hour about the guerrilla attacks, for which he claimed responsibility, and about his followers' willingness to be "martyrs" in the cause of resistance to the Israeli occupation.

Less than three weeks later, the building where the interview took place was blown up, killing the chieftain and about a dozen others, presumably the same aides we had seen. Wilkie remarked: "I hope they don't think we planted the bomb!"

War is hell, Sherman said. I agree.

## TERRORISM

Terrorism is one of the worst evils of the twentieth century. Television is one of the most remarkable phenomena of the twentieth century. The combination of television and terrorism confronts us with some of the knottiest ethical questions imaginable.

As a prelude to this discussion, terminology needs to be discussed. The word "terrorist" is a loosely used accusation, especially in the Middle East. "The problem," it has been pointed out, "is that your terrorist is my freedom fighter—and vice versa." We may define "terrorism" as the use of calculated violence against innocent civilians, often with a political objective. In the Middle East, the word "terrorist" has become synonymous for many Americans with "Arab" and "Palestinian." Israelis always refer to members of the Palestine Liberation Organization as "terrorists." On the other hand, the Israelis also called Lebanese "terrorists" even when these Lebanese were attacking Israeli military forces occupying southern Lebanon. Many journalists try to avoid use of the term "terrorist" in reporting acts of violence that have political implications; we simply identify the perpetrators as Palestinians or Israelis or whatever. If some other description is needed, we use the term "guerrilla."

Consider the following situations:

—A group of Japanese reporters and photographers stood around in Osaka, Japan, in June 1985 while two men broke into the apartment of an accused swindler and killed him with thirteen bayonet stabs. The TV cameras rolled all the while.

—Shiite Moslems hijacked a TWA airliner and kept its American passengers prisoners at the Beirut International Airport in June 1985. Charles Krauthammer wrote in an essay in *Time*,[5] ". . . during 17 days of astonishing symbiosis, television and terrorists co-produced—there is no better word—a hostage drama." ABC arranged with the Amal Shiites for an exclusive interview with the TWA pilot. The Amal held a news conference in which, I am told by colleagues who were there, the journalists leaped on top of tables and grew so unruly the Shiites had to delay the session. One of the aides at the U.S. Embassy shouted at the journalists, "You're worse than the f--- terrorists!"[6]

—After a group of terrorists led by Abul Abbas pirated the cruise liner *Achille Lauro* in the eastern Mediterranean in October 1985 and shot an American Jewish passenger, Leon Klinghoffer (by the way, the BBC did not identify Klinghoffer as a Jew—talk about missing the truth of a situation!) and pushed him overboard, NBC arranged to meet Abbas secretly and interview him.

—And my favorite: Jeff Price of the *Baltimore Sun*, my neighbor on the fourth floor at the Beit Agron in Jerusalem, told of being in Tripoli in April 1986 on the very day the United States made its air raid. As often is the case, the American journalists helped each other out, and Price's material was being transmitted over ABC lines. Jeff overheard a young producer in New York call in and ask, "Say, can you get Khadafy for 'Night Line'?" The young producer also asked, "He's Shiite, isn't he?" Whoever was taking the call said, "No, Greek Orthodox."

Such incidents have raised some serious questions: (1) Should the mass media allow themselves to be used as a megaphone for terrorists and their propaganda? (2) Specifically, should NBC have agreed to the condition in its interview with Abul Abbas that it not ask the most important question of all, "Where are you, Mr. Abbas?" For he had fled from Italian authorities and was a fugitive. (3) Last but not least, have the mass media invaded the privacy of innocent human beings by constant, adhesive-tape close coverage of the hostages and their families in what George Will has called "the pornography of grief"?[7] This happens frequently in the local media bent on getting "a local angle."

Some of the same issues involved in coverage of national security matters are involved here, as well, although the issues of national security are generally much more clear-cut. Referring to the TWA hijacking, former Secretary of State Henry A. Kissinger, violating his own strictures by being ubiquitous on television during the TWA hijack, told CBS, "It's a humiliation for the United States to have American citizens trotted out one by one, put on television, being forced to say they're being treated well."[8] After NBC's interview with Abbas, State Department spokesman Charles Redman said, "Obviously, terrorism thrives on this kind of publicity."[9] The *New York Times,* apparently, turned down Abbas' offer of an interview.[10] On the other hand, Hamilton Jordan, who played key behind-the-scenes roles during the Iranian hostage crisis, claimed that TV is helpful because the terrorists must keep the hostages alive in order to guarantee continuing coverage.[11] Howard Stringer, executive vice president of CBS News, also said that TV "made it hard to kill the hostages or even to keep them." It also makes the media too much a part of the story. Said Karen Elliott House, foreign editor of the *Wall Street Journal:* "We are not in the business of spreading propaganda but in the business of analyzing why things happen and what they mean."[12] Bryant Gumbel, of NBC's "Today Show," told Peggy Seay, the sister of Terry Anderson, a hostage in Lebanon, "We'll keep your story up front." David Hartman, of "Good Morning, America," asked the Lebanese Shiite leader, Nabih Berri, "Any final words to President Reagan this morning?"[13]

How do we handle these matters? There are two ways:

The first is government censorship. One problem of government censorship, as we have seen, is that it is often used to cover up wrongdoing or malfeasance.

But in the United States freedom of the press is guaranteed in the

First Amendment, and it is an almost absolute freedom. Consequently, any censorship by the American media must be self-imposed. CBS commentator Charles Osgood summed it up this way: "The news media should not be government controlled . . . but perhaps we should not let Abul Abbas and his kind call the shots either."[14]

Thus, some form of self-censorship provides the second way for handling the problems involved in news gathering about terrorism. What ought to guide us in handling such matters? (I have found very few if any formulas offered for making decisions of this kind, and the suggestions offered here are mine and mine alone.)

We must do some ethical analysis. Consider our values. Should one always tell the truth? Yes. That is an important value. Should you always obey your parents? Yes, another important value. Should one cause emotional pain to another person? No. Yet another important value. But we have said that often values, important values, collide, and then we are forced to make a choice. For instance, do we tell aged parents something that we know will cause them pain? Does one spouse tell the other, emotionally fragile spouse that he or she has had an affair? Such an expression of honesty may make the guilty party feel cleansed, but it may also transfer the burden for dealing with the matter to a person who does not have the resources to do so. The does *not* mean we have discarded the value of truth. It *does* mean that two important values have come into conflict, and we were forced to choose one over the other.

So, terrorism seems to bring the value of telling the truth into conflict with the value of preserving human lives. John Seigenthaler, editorial page editor of *USA Today* and Robert F. Kennedy's former aide, acknowledged this dilemma. Commenting on the NBC interview with Abbas, Seigenthaler said, "What the journalist has to consider is whether the information to be gained is so vital that it tips the scale in favor of granting protection to a fugitive."[15] Charles Krauthammer noted the fascination and indispensability that evil has for journalism, and said, "The question is how to fix on the subject without merging with it."[16]

The key is truth. As has often been said, we are not obliged always to tell the full truth but we are obliged not to tell a lie. So, one solution frequently is to tell only that part of the truth that would not cause harm.

But I think we can go beyond this. As we have noted, truth is invariably linked to justice and peace. Here is the clue. We also have noted that facts are not necessarily synonymous with truth. The journalist's obligation is to truth, not mere facts. Therefore, the journalist's obligation is to pursue those stories that will contribute to justice and peace.

Would publication of a story provoke the terrorists and thus endanger lives? That surely would be a disruption of peace, and that story ought not to be printed. Should the strategy of the authorities be disclosed in a story, thus alerting the terrorists to take counter-measures? Again, that story hardly would contribute to justice and peace and ought not to be printed. Should the press print the demands of the terrorists? In the case of the TWA hijackers, they were demanding release of four hundred Lebanese Shiites held prisoner in Israel contrary to the Geneva Convention prohibiting taking prisoners of war into another country, a clear case of justice. I think it was appropriate to print or broadcast those demands.

It is quite clear that beyond the broad principle of disseminating only those stories that contribute to justice and peace, there are few specific rules, requiring that almost each situation and each story be judged on its merits.

One may ask, but how many journalists would approach a terrorist act in this fashion? As Jonathan Alter wrote in *Newsweek*,[17] "In war, reporters have to make up their own guidelines, often under fire. Ethical distinctions are sometimes the first casualty." This simply demonstrates the need for more journalists and consumers to wrestle with the ethics of news.

Further, we all are members of the human family before we are journalists. In situations like terrorism, we must remember that our obligation is first of all to people, not to the story.

CHAPTER 10

# Watergate

It was the campaign year 1972. Richard M. Nixon was seeking a second term, and was surrounded by men determined to assure it happened. For a brief moment in the polls in June, George McGovern had edged ahead of Nixon.

In June, five men, acting on orders from on high, broke into the Democratic national offices in the Watergate complex in Washington and planted electronic eavesdropping devices. Their purpose remains unclear to this day. Except for the *Washington Post*, CBS, the *Los Angeles Times* and a few others, the scandal went largely unprobed until March 1973, when the cover-up started to unravel and the news organizations, all at once, assigned full-time reporters. I experienced this first hand. Talk about deeper implications of the Watergate "caper," as it was known initially, was rife around Washington at the time of the Republican convention in Miami Beach in late August. I was left in charge of the UPI Washington bureau during the convention, and I assigned a reporter full time to the Watergate affair. Many of the staff took vacations after the convention, and while they were coming back, I was assigned to cover the McGovern campaign, starting on Labor Day. When I returned two weeks later, I found that the reporter I had assigned to Watergate had been taken off the story. UPI did not assign a reporter full time to Watergate until I was put on the story the following March, seven months later. What if UPI had kept a reporter on Watergate, thus forcing the AP and others to follow suit? The scandal might have been broken far, far sooner.

The scandal revealed the distrust, zeal, and utter pragmatism that had festered in the White House and the Committee to Reelect the President. When the cover-up came unglued, the tightly knit team that had put loyalty above all else turned on each other with a vengeance. It created the most serious internal crisis in the federal government since the Civil War. Worse, it caused the people of America to have deep suspicions about the basic institutions of their government—and made mockery of the Constitution and the Bill of Rights.

During the height of the crisis, one key official remarked to me and UPI colleague Clay Richards that we had no idea how the U.S. government had slowed almost to a halt. It was impossible, he said, to get quick action on even so routine a procedure as approval of a new stamp.

## The Moral Dimension

In March 1983, when the media finally awakened, we reported in excruciating detail about the break-in, the White House tapes, Richard Nixon's finances and his language. Seldom if ever has a public official been put under the media's X-ray scrutiny as much as he was. But we were much less skillful in defining *why* Watergate happened, what it is that makes those who have power so vulnerable to abusing it, so greedy in wanting to expand it. These were moral questions critical to understanding Watergate, and we dealt with them inadequately, if at all.

The late Sen. Sam J. Ervin Jr., D-N.C., chairman of the Senate Watergate committee, was the great moral interpreter of the Watergate ordeal. During the 1973 hearings, time and again he took some of the cynical testimony he heard and put it into a moral framework. His committee elicited testimony from Bart Porter, the young, self-confident scheduling director for the Committee to Reelect the President. Quoting Shakespeare, Ervin told the brash young man: "Had I but served my God with half the zeal I served my king, he would not in mine age have left me naked to mine enemies."[1] Ervin quoted Jesus in saying that men prefer darkness when their deeds are evil.[2] Watergate was the story of men—and always they were men—who made misleading statements and invoked a false sense of national security to hide the truth.

Sometimes I asked Watergate defendants in the sidewalk news conferences we held outside U.S. District Courthouse in Washington whether they felt any remorse. Invariably, they scorned the question, indicating the moral bankruptcy that characterized the administration at that time.

A short time after the news of his conversion to Christ became public in late 1973, I interviewed Charles W. Colson, who had been White House special counsel and Nixon's political operative. The interview moved in question-and-answer on our prime UPI "A" wire, one of the longest dispatches ever carried on a spot story. As the interview came to a close, I asked Colson what the sin of Watergate was. He paused, and finally answered. "Arrogance was the great sin of Watergate." Millions of words have been written about Watergate, but Colson's half-dozen words came closest to capturing the truth.

The Watergate scandal, cracked largely through the persistence of two young reporters, demonstrated the purging effect of truth finally uncovered. The subsequent televising of the 1973 Senate hearings and the 1974 House Judiciary impeachment inquiry finally led to the unraveling of the Watergate cover-up and the resignation of Richard Nixon. The people might have distrusted mere press and television accounts of those proceedings. But through the television cameras the people were able to see and hear John Dean, John Mitchell, H.R. Haldeman, John Ehrlichman, Charles Colson, and others—and draw their own conclusions about whether the witnesses were telling the truth.

There was a critical moral dimension to Watergate, but there was also a way in which Watergate exemplified some far-reaching changes in America that went far beyond the break-in at the Democratic National Committee. These were the scandals involving the Associated Milk Producers Inc. (AMPI) and International Telephone and Telegraph (ITT).

If the break-in at the Democratic national headquarters demonstrated the moral climate in America, the AMPI and ITT scandals demonstrated the economic and social revolution. All fell under the general rubric called "Watergate"; all of the cases were handled by the Special Watergate Prosecutor Force.

## AMPI and ITT: The Economic and Social Revolution

To explain how the AMPI and ITT scandals burst onto the scene during the Nixon administration, it is necessary to review some history. There has been a profound inability on the part of the press to deal adequately with the great winds of change that have revolutionized this country in the last few generations. A revolution does not necessarily require the spilling of blood; rather, a revolution is a tearing inside out.

Indeed, my childhood experiences presaged the national convulsions that were to come with Watergate. While I was growing up on an Iowa farm, my father milked fifteen to twenty cows twice a day, poured the milk into ten-gallon cans, and put them in an outdoor stock tank to cool. Each morning, Jack Williams came by in his Ford V-8 truck, its slatboard box rattling, to pick up the milk and take it to the Sweet Clover Dairy, one of a half-dozen small dairies in Mason City. My sister Lois and her friends helped work their way through college by hand-wrapping butter at another Mason City dairy, Iowa State Brand Creameries Inc. It was an immaculate sight—rows of young women in white uniforms, taking pounds or quarter pounds of butter off a conveyor belt, and wrapping them quickly and crisply. Eventually, the Sweet Clover Dairy and the Iowa State Brand Creameries and uncounted other dairies just like them sold out or were merged several times over. Finally, all of those dairies became Associated Milk Producers Inc. (AMPI), a cooperative dairy so large that it processed a sizeable fraction of all the milk drunk between Minnesota and Mexico.

Watergate's so-called "milk fund" scandal was the story of AMPI's promise of a $2 million contribution to the 1972 Nixon campaign, presumably in expectation of obtaining a raise in the federal price support for raw milk. The support price was increased—and the campaign got the contribution.

In similar ways, another childhood experience helped me understand the ITT case. My parents shopped at the Sam Raizes Department Store in Mason City. The store was vital to our existence as a family. My parents sold eggs to the store in exchange for groceries and other items. There, my mother bought my bib-overalls—I called them "over-hauls." After high school classes were over, I stopped in to buy a snack. The store is now closed and city folk take their business to some of the shopping malls on the edge of town. I and most of my friends helped work our way through college by working summers at Jacob E. Decker and Sons, a family-owned packing plant that had been bought out by Armour. Eventually, Armour was bought out by Greyhound, and in its corporate headquarters in Phoenix, Ariz., a few years later, the decision was made to close down Deckers. I have no idea now where Mason City youth go to find summer work. The packing plant that helped so many students get through college was closed down, the result of an impersonal corporate decision made 1,500 miles away.

The story of the International Telephone and Telegraph Co. (ITT) and how its astronomic growth had led to crime was revealed. A few years earlier, ITT had been a relatively small firm doing much of its business abroad. It grew to mammoth proportions by buying Avis rental cars, Sheraton hotels, Canteen food vending machines, Continental Baking, Grinnell water sprinklers, Hartford Insurance, and many other firms. It had become a giant. It was so strong that it was accused during Watergate of obtaining a favorable antitrust settlement from the Justice Department by promising the Nixon campaign $400,000-worth of services at a new hotel in San Diego.

## The Challenge

Watergate presented huge challenges to the media. In no other area of reporting are journalists tempted to excess and skirting the law as in investigative journalism. But reporters must adhere to the same strict standards themselves that their stories demand of the suspect or target of the investigation.

# CHAPTER 11

# Briefly, and Finally . . .

There are countless situations in which the journalist faces ethical problems. The ones discussed in separate chapters of this book were experienced personally by the author. Here are others, which the writer also has covered from time to time.


## RELIGION


Nowhere are stereotypes bandied about quite so freely as in the case of religious people, especially conservatives.

### Evangelical View of the World

The Fundamentalist and Evangelical Christian community, distorting the Scripture that calls on them to "come ye apart and be ye separate," often assigns to hell anyone who does not agree with them theologically. In recent years, this litmus test of doctrinal purity as defined by them has been extended to political issues. Anyone who favored establishment of a U.S. Department of Education, ratification of the Panama Canal treaties, the use of school busing for desegregation purposes, and opposed compulsory school prayer and a constitutional amendment banning abortions was not a true Christian. If the Fundamentalist Christians really want to damn a person, in their view, they call that person a "secular humanist."

I believe there are two reasons for this: (1) a narrow view of the breadth of the Christian message, and (2) an underestimation of the power of the truth of the gospel. The Fundamentalists' fears actually reflect a lack of the faith they claim.

## The World's View of Evangelicals

On the other hand, the liberal politicians and many journalists scoff at and ridicule Fundamentalist Christians. Fundamentalist Christian women typically are pictured in TV clips as overweight and Fundamentalist men always wear polyester suits.

As Pat Robertson, the founder of the Christian Broadcasting Network and host of its "700 Club," prepared to run for the Republican nomination for president, the television networks hauled out years-old clips of him praying for the healing of hemorrhoids and psoriasis. Finally, James M. Wall, a political opponent of Robertson and editor of a theologically liberal magazine, *The Christian Century*, wrote in protest that the early press treatment of Robertson was nothing less than "religious bigotry."[1]

There are two reasons for this as well: (1) a gross ignorance about basic Christianity on the part of many in the mass media, and (2) a lack of fairness by demanding that Fundamentalists and Evangelicals be completely pure and above reproach.

## Definitions and Background

Worse, historical terminology is butchered. The term *Fundamentalist* dates to the early 1900s, when five points emerged as "fundamental" to the faith—the virgin birth of Jesus Christ, His physical resurrection, the infallibility of the Bible, the atonement by Christ on the Cross, and the physical Second Coming of Christ. Although this has nothing to do with their basic beliefs, Fundamentalists are socially somewhat removed from the rest of the world. They generally do not drink, do not swear, do not smoke, do not go to movies, and do not dance. Their friends are drawn from their religious circle. Jerry Falwell is a Fundamentalist.

Evangelicals believe doctrinally what Fundamentalists believe, although they may not adhere quite as tightly to the literal inerrancy of the Bible. But socially, they are much more open in their contacts and free in their behavior. Wheaton College and Fuller Seminary are evangelical institutions.

Charismatics or Pentecostals are Christians who come from the whole range of Protestant denominations as well as Catholicism and who emphasize an experience of the Holy Spirit that leads them to speak in tongues, believe in healings, and worship with upraised hands. Pat Robertson is a charismatic.

All three groups emphasize a personal experience of Jesus Christ. Altogether, there are an estimated sixty million of these faithful in the United States.

Historically, there was a long period of silence in the mass media's coverage of Fundamental and Evangelicals. Whatever coverage there was was of celebrities and public people who had dramatic conversion experiences.

In 1970, I interviewed Windsor Elliott, one of the nation's top fashion models, with many magazine covers to her credit. She had been converted to Christ and had given up her career in order to try to win other young professionals to faith. A striking color picture of the beautiful young woman accompanied the dispatch. The *Florida Times-Union* and *Jacksonville Journal* ran the story and picture on page one and were flooded with letters and telephone calls from readers. "I can hardly think of anything we've done in years and years that has so touched a nerve as did this UPI yard," *Times-Union* managing editor Bruce Manning said. "Perhaps there is a gnawing hunger abroad for a taste of the wholesome and good will. But whatever it is, we are grateful for the response . . ."[2]

In 1974, Charles Colson's story, *Born Again* (a title he says he found in his wife's Catholic hymnal) was published, and in 1976, Jimmy Carter's born-again experience became public. The phrase, "born again," comes from the New Testament (John 3:3). The mass media's handling of it showed great ignorance and occasional hostility. I have cited a television anchorman saying it was "not a bizarre, mountaintop experience, but one common to many millions of Americans," and Jody Powell's conclusion that the American people understood that aspect of Carter's life better than the reporters.

There was a parallel growth of political conservatism and religious conservatism in the United States, and a surge of Fundamentalist affluence and acceptance. Soon, it seemed, everyone was "born again," especially candidates for political office. "Born again" became a cliché used in ads and political campaigns that have no other relationship whatsoever to the original meaning. "And what about the incorrect, and often pejorative, use of the word 'fundamentalist,' which has come to mean anyone behaving in a fanatical manner?" asks Cal Thomas, a syndicated columnist and a Fundamentalist Christian.[3]

If the 1988 political campaign was "the year of character," it also was the year of "the fallen televangelists."

The media covered the sins and life styles of Jim and Tammy Bakker and Jimmy Swaggart and their brethren in embarrassing detail. The saturation coverage was entirely appropriate, as I have suggested earlier. The trust of many of the faithful was invested in these evangelists, and it was a trust that was broken.

It is ironic—and a glaring fact that ought to lead the so-called religious press to some rigorous self-examination—that the secular press and not the religious press was the prophet in calling the evangelists to account for their sins. In fact, the religious press could not decide how to cover their brethren. One minister, under threat of blackmail, confessed to adultery and resigned the presidency of a large religious organization. Then, the minister requested a religious magazine, on whose board he sat, to interview him on "why I committed adultery." The magazine agreed. It was a tasteless sequel to a tragic affair.

# Social Issues

My beat while I was covering Congress during the first two and a half years of the Reagan administration was the so-called "social" issues—abortion, pornography, school prayer, and school busing for desegregation purposes. This was the agenda of the New Right, often identified with the Fundamentalists. Few things inspired such heat on both sides as these issues.

I found these approaches to be helpful:

—Be fair. It was not required that every story be balanced, because occasionally a single story was designed to treat a single aspect. But the overall coverage ought to be.

—Use precise, unemotional language. Don't describe someone as being "pro-abortion" when this person merely favors the right to have an abortion. "Pro-life" is almost as fuzzy a word.

—Talk to both sides and attribute honest motives to each. Many in the mass media feel uncomfortable talking to opponents of abortion and often take a slightly condescending approach.

—Do thorough reporting. In the case of pornography, for instance, the 1970 report of the Commission on Pornography read very differently from the conservative conclusions of the commission that reported during the Reagan administration. The 1970 report concluded that pornographic literature actually deadens sexual drives, so it proposed the repeal of all laws regulating the distribution and possession of "explicit sexual material" to adults. These conclusions were rarely referred to in coverage of the later report. In the case of welfare fraud, thorough reporting would reveal that most crimes were committed by businesses, not recipients. Thorough reporting helps destroy the myths that often surround volatile issues.

## SPORTS AND THE ARTS

The best advice for handling sports stories was given me by Ed Sainsbury, the veteran UPI Central Division sports editor: Handle a game like you would any other news story. This is the day of "second-day leads" and different approaches to writing sports. Often the writing is little more than cheerleading for the home team. The stories are written in such a self-conscious way by the sports reporter that they are mushy and lack the fundamental detail of who won and how. It ought to be an unwritten rule that the *final score* and a significant detail like the top individual performance be included in at least the first or second paragraph of a story.

"Don't be a fan! Don't be a fan!" Sainsbury used to shout. Sports writers make political writers look like pikers in the ways in which they overpsychologize the players and analyze every detail of the process. One way to deal with this might be to knock down the false wall that exists between sports writers and other reporters. Perhaps sports writers should be part of the general staff, rotated from assignment to assignment. On the other hand, in coverage and criticism of the arts perhaps more than any other area, the expertise of the reporter comes into question: How much background in music, or drama, or the ballet has the reporter had? An additional thought: Why should the professional teams hold veto power over their play-by-play announcers?

Too often the sports pages run the box scores and a lot of rah-rah or boo-boo—it seems to be one or the other—for the home team. In the process, critical areas—related to justice and peace—are being overlooked by sports writers. Why has more not been done about violence in sports, especially in hockey? Why has more not been written about the supersalaries in sports? about the absence of blacks in professional management? about participatory sports, as contrasted to the coverage of spectator sports?

It was in the area of cultural affairs, paradoxically, that I had my greatest enjoyment but was least at ease ethically. I am from Mason City, Iowa, home of Meredith Willson and his "River City" of *The Music Man* fame. I had played in the award-winning band and brass quintet, and I had my key from the University of Iowa bands. But I knew little about ballet or drama, except for a short role in Thornton Wilder's *The Skin of Our Teeth* in the Sioux Falls Community Theater. The Kennedy Center for the Performing Arts opened in Washington in 1971, and I helped cover it for UPI. That began a decade in which I did most of the cultural affairs writings for UPI in Washington. I was not a critic or a reviewer; rather, for the most part, I conducted interviews.

And what an array I interviewed! I interviewed Mikhail Baryshnikov soon after his defection, and was amazed that this perfect physical specimen chain-smoked. I interviewed Victor Borge and we wound up talking about what humor is. I interviewed Ernest Thompson, the young playwright, and when the conversation turned to his parents and grandparents, I understood why he wrote *On Golden Pond*. There were also Mary Martin, the director-general of the Bolshoi Ballet, the leading Japanese kibuki dancer and a host of others.

I often found that asking about the star's early years caused them to open up and get away from the clichéd answer. This got me my favorite story; although a bit humorous, it involved some serious points. It was an interview with Elizabeth Ashley.

I made an appointment to interview her in her dressing room at the Kennedy Center, where she was performing. Our photographer, who shall go unnamed, arranged to be there as well. I arrived a few minutes late, and the photographer was already there. Ashley, her hair straight, no makeup, blue-tinted glasses, and clad in an old pair of khaki slacks, was unprepared for him. They were arguing. "The last thing the world needs is another eight-by-ten glossy of Elizabeth Ashley," she said. Back and forth it went. Finally, the photographer said, "Look, lady, I work nine-to-five and it just happens that in that time I'm supposed to take a picture of you."

The pictures he finally took were unusable. The interview got off similarly. "Are you married now?" I asked, uncertain. "Yes," she said tersely. "To whom?" I asked. "You don't know him," she retorted. Then, I asked her about her early years. She noticeably softened. I learned her mother had been a government clerk-typist in Louisiana. Soon Elizabeth was talking freely and openly, and the interview went beyond my allotted time. She told me about a shouting match she had had that morning with a garage attendant. She recounted the incident, complete with raised voice and profanity.

We both realized it was getting late and she said, "I've got to get dressed now for the performance." I thanked her and left. Hovering outside the door of her dressing room, nervously smoking a cigarette, was the Kennedy Center's Leo Sullivan. "What happened?" he asked. "I got off to a rocky start but it went great," I said. "I knew she was in a bad mood and when I came down and heard her shouting and swearing, I was afraid of what had happened," Leo replied.

I wrote the interview, complete with her abundant profanity. She had asked to see the story so I sent her a copy (something which I have never objected to doing, because it allows me to correct any errors. I always insist on the right of my own perspective in the story.) Soon afterward, my phone rang. "This is Elizabeth Ashley," the voice said, talking a mile a minute. I was covering Watergate at the time, and in that frame of mind, I thought she said, "Elizabeth Holtzman," a member of the House Judiciary Committee. Once I switched modes, I realized Ashley was pointing out the story was accurate but was asking me to remove the profanity. "Why? You said it," I replied. Her response was interesting— and maybe even valid. "It distracts people from the point I'm trying to make, and besides, it makes my mother feel bad." We agreed that I would remove all but one swear word to show that she did indeed use that kind of language. Later, despite this precaution, a San Francisco newspaper carried a letter to the editor protesting the use of that one word.

I was reminded again that as a reporter, dealing with people in the public eye can be very difficult. Entertainers finally aren't much different than politicians—or vice versa. The reporter is presented the temptation of rubbing shoulders with the luminous and the challenge of getting to the core of who the person really is.

My interviews with Deborah Kerr were vastly different from that with Elizabeth Ashley—and warmer. I had seen her in *Tea and Sympathy* in Minneapolis in 1955. When I interviewed her in Washington a quarter of a century later, I told her about that and it seemed to touch her. Our photographer, as always, snapped a picture of the two of us. We were sitting in her dressing room. I was gesturing as if asking a question and she had a slight smile on her face. Bob Andrews, one of my colleagues, later saw the photo and taped on some cutlines that said, "No, Mr. Pippert or whatever your name is, I most definitely will *not* consent to a roll in the hay." Some time later, I interviewed her again. I brought along the photo for her to autograph, and I told her about Andrews' comic cutlines. She laughed warmly and signed it. Later I glanced at what she had written: "For Wes—and I *don't* mean what it looks like I'm saying!!!"

Perhaps my use of these "war stories" in this section betrays my own avoidance in dealing with a central ethical issue. Why should not a publication pay its reporter's way into games and performances? Why should reporters be given huge spreads of food and drinks at big sporting events and be guests at special receptions for performing artists? I confess that many, many times I have been the recipient of such "freebies." How much, subtly, does this make the journalist feel beholden to the performer or host team? In short, *all* journalists, including me, ought to pay our way in.

## AGRICULTURE AND BUSINESS

In a day of mergers and acquisitions, corporations are getting bigger and more powerful. In fact, we have no idea of the extent of influence these corporations have on the average person. I discussed this in some detail in the chapter on Watergate. These corporations do most of their business in secrecy. We know far more about the political process in America than we do about the corporate process.

Perhaps the mass media ought to wage an attack to open up coverage of the board rooms and multibillion-dollar transactions to the public, as difficult as that may be. Tom Brokaw, the NBC anchorman, compared the seriousness of the trading scandal to Watergate in the previous decade. Yet, far less is likely ever to be known about Wall Street than Watergate.

This is the story of AMPI and the Sweet Clover Dairy, of ITT and the Sam Raizes Department Store, of Greyhound and Jacob E. Decker and Sons. It also is the story of Goodyear Rubber. Pete Geiger of the *Akron Beacon Journal* describes how one newspaper covered a corporate raid:

> In October 1986, corporate raider James M. Goldsmith, with the help of Merrill Lynch, made a raid on Goodyear Tire & Rubber Co. The company circled its wagons, telling employees not to talk to the press.
>
> An *Akron Beacon Journal* reporter staked out Goodyear's world headquarters building in Akron, waiting in the lobby for executives to leave work. Security guards told the reporter he'd have to leave, so he and a photographer stood in the freezing rain on the sidewalk in front of the building, asking each executive who left to say what was going on inside.
>
> Almost to a man, each declined, explaining he'd been told to avoid just such a reporter asking just such questions. But one man, a corporate accountant, asked if his identity could be protected. He gave a reporter his home phone number, saying there was indeed a story that needed to be told.
>
> The editors of the *Beacon Journal* never learned the executive's name. But for many nights thereafter, from his phone at home, he painted the picture of a corporation that, in an effort to diversify, to stake its future on

more than one line of products, had built a conglomerate whose parts were worth more, taken individually, than was the value of all its stock taken in sum.

Thus the raider's intent became obvious despite his disclaimers: Sell off the various divisions, pocket the profits and leave the weakened tire company to limp into the future diminished. He had done as much to other corporations.

As this anonymous accountant painted the broad picture, as his words began appearing in the newspaper, others began to open up with sobering details:

—the divisions most likely to be sold off

—the numbers of employees that would be affected

—the total purchasing power lost

—the economic "multiplier" effect on the community

—and the corporation's charity contributions and tax revenues that might be lost.

The community reacted in outrage as the details became known. Various organizations and individuals began buying Goodyear stock. Rallies were staged. And the Ohio General Assembly, ever alert to popular ground-swells, drafted antitakeover legislation.

Goldsmith, the raider, bowed out of the fight, taking $93 million "greenmail" and citing the impossibility of continuing in the face of the impending state legislation.

Now, other companies under raid come to Goodyear for advice on how to cope. And the *Beacon Journal* won the 1987 Pulitzer Prize in general news reporting for its coverage of the entire raid, its effects and its aftermath. Many reporters contributed to the coverage and the prize was awarded to the staff.[4]

The corporate world of takeovers and high finance now has invaded agriculture, once the main business and way of life in America. For generations, agriculture was a family business. No longer.

No one covers the issues of agriculture better than Paul Pippert, one of the nation's senior farm broadcasters and my brother. One of his stories won the 1978 "Oscar in Agriculture," funded by the DeKalb Research Corporation and endorsed by the National Association of Farm Broadcasters. The story involved the government's attempt to take 2,500 acres of prime farm land known as "Jackass Bend" thirty miles east of Kansas City for a wildlife refuge. His eight-minute tape included interviews with a congressman, a farmer, the Army Engineers, and his own analysis of the dispute as "the war to keep farm land in production." Ten years later, Jackass Bend was still farm land. As discussed in chapter 5, we still do not pay adequate attention to what is happening to the family farm and the society that surrounded it; we are not paying enough attention to the impact of agribusiness on the typical farmer. Movies, notably *Country* with Jessica Lange, helped capture the emotional duress burdening the farm family as a result of farm prices that have stayed low while farm costs have skyrocketed, complicated by such hard-nosed financial institutions as the Federal Land Bank.

Dr. Gary Comstock, a philosopher at Iowa State University, has written:

> Glance through any issue of *Successful Farming, Wallace's Farmer,* or *Landowner.* You will see thousands of advertisements heralding the advent of the most recent miracle seed or plow. You will see editorials and articles hawking the latest in technological breakthrough. You will not see charts comparing the relative success rates of various seeds. You will not see angry stories unmasking the pretensions of the latest claims for fertilizer. You will not see critical assessments of combines and tractors. You will not find muck-raking journalists uncovering illegal working conditions at IBP's beef-packing plants, exposing the levels of nitrate contaminants in northeast Iowa well-water, or presenting the latest predictions about the number of farmers that will go under from recent breakthroughs in biotechnology. Every line is praise of this or that "advance," so that the line between paid advertisements and journalistic reporting is almost indistinguishable.[5]

## LOCAL JOURNALISM

My sister and I were talking by transoceanic telephone one day near the end of my tour in Israel. How have you liked it, Marie asked. Oh, I said, I've loved it more than any assignment I ever had. Then, without pausing, I added, well, maybe not as much as my assignment in South Dakota. I meant it as a joke, but as I thought about it, I knew that there was a germ of truth in what I had said. In many ways, my assignment in Sioux Falls and Pierre was the favorite of my career.

The opportunities in local journalism can be as exciting and as fulfilling as those anywhere else in the world, including Washington and a foreign assignment. There is one key reason: local situations are small enough that one can be a reporter in the fullest sense of the word, keeping abreast of situations, knowing the players, feeling that one has a handle on what is going on. But local journalists confront more temptations and ethically murky problems than other journalists.

Locally, the coming of television has drastically affected newspapers in many ways. As noted already, TV has hurt afternoon newspapers the most. What could an afternoon newspaper report that would be news to the person getting home from work in late afternoon and turning on the slick, well-produced network news shows? What could an afternoon newspaper report, that as a matter of fact, had not already been in the morning newspaper?

My own impression of local TV news is that it suffers from the schizophrenia of trying to be both entertainment and journalism. It has no clear standards for ranking news stories in order of importance: for instance, is the weather overreported? It strains to be chatty, with these multianchor desks. The anchors hold pencils in their hands, but did you ever see them write with them? Or, there is the jacket off, the necktie loosened, the collar unbuttoned, the studied casual "on-the-job-and-working" appearance for the one-minute cut-aways during the evening.

Someone remarked that printed journalism (newspapers and magazines) is several hundred years old. It therefore is quite mature and we see it in its finest form in the *New York Times*, the *Washington Post*, the *Boston Globe*. Television journalism is little more than a generation old, a mere infant compared to printed journalism. This may be one reason for its immaturity.

There is an intimacy to local journalism that is both its blessing and its curse, but I think this intimacy makes local journalism the most exciting of all.

*1. The blessing.*    In South Dakota, I was one of three reporters covering the State Capitol on a regular basis. We drank coffee on the ground floor of the Capitol, often with an assistant attorney general if not the attorney general himself, the curriculum specialist from the Department of Public Instruction, the secretary of state, two or three state agents. I knew everyone personally on a first-name basis. Joe Foss, the World War II flying ace and one of the country's best raconteurs, was governor. One time he learned we both had to be at the Harrold, S.D., High School graduation. "I'll pick you up," he said. He did—and he did the driving himself.

I have never been so confident that I had a grip on the story, as I was in South Dakota as a reporter in my early twenties—surely not years later in Washington, which was much too big and complex; surely not in Israel, although I felt I had a better grasp on what was going on in Israel than I did in Washington even while covering the White House. A reporter needs to know what is going on, and whenever I have listened to a local journalist I have always felt a bit of envy.

*2. The curse.*    The dark side of small-town intimacy is that it often brings tremendous pressure to bear on the reporter or editor by forces that want to suppress or shape truth according to their own wishes or whims.

While I was covering Watergate in 1973 and 1974, I got two calls from acquaintances in widely separated places. Both, unknown to one another, used the same expression: "mini-Watergates" were going on in their hometowns. The powerful people in a town—the mayor, the police chief, the real estate baron—often have enormous influence on a local editor. There is no doubt that cover-ups are more frequent and easier to execute in a locality where there may be only one editor than in a city like New York or Washington where there is is intense media competition. You tell me—which is more likely to be hushed up, the drug arrest of the president's son or the mayor's son? Often, the local editor himself wields power perhaps simply through being established and on the scene a long time. The *Des Moines Register* and the *Washingtonion* magazine carried a series on the most powerful people in Des Moines and the wealthiest people in Washington, respectively. What amazed me was the number of names I did not recognize. A lot of powerful people are going unreported throughout the United States—which is probably exactly the way they want it.

There is a paradox here. It's a great irony that what little trust people do have in the mass media is often misplaced. When people condemn the mass media, they generally mean the big newspapers and television networks. They tend to be much more trusting of the local paper, because it is closer to them. Intimacy is a product of proximity as well as of emotional rapport.

This chapter demonstrates that *any* news beat or assignment has ethical questions attached to it. At the same time, if there are moral challenges involved, there also are opportunities to pursue issues of justice and peace in each of these stories. And in doing so, we may have discovered truth, and that it has helped set us free.

# Appendix 1
# Writing

## News writing and other forms of writing

The main difference between journalistic writing, or news, and other kinds of writing has traditionally been the element of *timeliness*, with the latest development generally expressed in the lead. But even feature stories are pegged to a timely angle. There seems to be less difference these days between journalistic and other kinds of writing, perhaps as a result of television: fewer people get the *latest* news from their daily newspapers so newspapers must take a different approach. There is now a tendency to write the broad lead rather than one specifically tied to "today." Many sports stories demonstrate an attempt, not yet perfected, to get beyond the tradition of giving the score and telling how the winning run or point was scored.

Hoover Cott, who published a weekly newspaper in Kansas for twenty years, said, "It is one of my few regrets that I did not have more time to employ, to exploit, to expand and enjoy the creativity, the power and charm of the written word" (personal correspondence, 30 June 1983).

## Reading and writing

The real secret to good writing is good reading. Walter Steigelman, my professor at the University of Iowa, used to say: "Read everything, even if it's merely the back of the cereal box, but read." Especially, read your own writing. Read and reread. I have yet to reread a story without finding more words to knock out. Read it aloud. If it sounds okay, chances are it will read okay. Others may disagree, but I think there is little difference between the written and the spoken word. The biggest challenge I ever had was in South Dakota, where the same UPI wire went to both newspapers and radio stations. I had to wr..e in such a way that the story would be clear as heard in a newscast or read in a newspaper.

## Write like you talk

Think and write Anglo-Saxon, not Latin derivatives; earthy, not cerebral. All cuss words, which are easily understood, are one-syllable Anglo-Saxon words! The story of David and Goliath (1 Sam. 17) is made up of one-syllable words.

Use the active voice, not the passive.

Use powerful verbs, do not use adjectives and adverbs. "Dike Edelman returned the opening kickoff 98 yards Saturday to detonate an Illinois explosion that demolished Michigan, 48-0."

Use quotes. Did you ever notice that one likes to read the dialogue in novels more than the detail? If possible, use full quotes. If one uses a fragmentary quote in the lead, include the full quote in the body of the story.

## Write simply and clearly

Use simple sentences. One of the most effective ways to assure this is to keep your sentences to no more than two or three lines. Split your sentence into two if it gets compound or too long. When quoting, use "said." Almost any synonym tends to color the quote.

Be terse. The busyness of the world, the information explosion, the competing demands for people's attention mean you can't engage in verbal excess.

A major barrier to clear writing is making it too complex. Keep it simple. The challenge is to discuss complex matters in simple ways. If the subject matter is very complicated, tell it chronologically. The Creation story, three hundred words, is a masterpiece illustrating this. My colleague, Gerald Nadler, wrote about Lebanon: "Most countries are a people before they become a nation; Lebanon was a nation before it became a people." "The Bedouin are as far removed from the tent these days as the American Indian is from the teepee." "The Druze are about as far removed from Islam as Christianity is from Judaism."

## The Lead

When wrestling with the lead, think to yourself, how would I say this to a friend? how would I write this in a ten-word telegram? how would I write a headline for this story? These tips may give you the clue to a simple lead.

The two points of emphasis in any sentence are the first and last. Tuck insignificant detail into the middle of the sentence.

Francis T. Leary, the late managing editor of UPI, said that occupations have no place in the lead, unless they are central to the story. For instance, the occupation is irrelevant in the following: "A forty-three-year-old jeweler was killed today when his car hit a bridge on Interstate 270." But the occupation would be relevant in this story: "A butcher clubbed his wife to death today with a meat cleaver, police said."

Look for an angle. Often the angle is historical, and the *New York Times* especially likes this. When the White House was given a simple paint job, I wrote that it was the biggest project since the renovation during the Truman administration. The *Times* used the story. My first boss, Richard McFarland, told me: "Write about things that will make people sitting in bars talk about them."

While I was in the UPI Chicago bureau, our police reporter, Robert T. Laughran, who had covered Chicago's finest for forty-nine years, phoned in the details of an unusual, but relatively minor, crime. A burglar had cut himself severely while trying to break into a store. He wandered off bleeding profusely, collapsed and died a block or two away. Early the next morning, simultaneously, a passerby discovered the body and called homicide police, and the storekeeper discovered the break-in and called burglary detectives. Both sets of police discovered the blood and started tracking it. UPI's David Smother's wrote:

> Chicago (UPI)—Chicago's homicide and burglary detectives met today along a path of blood.

I remember one incident vividly because it was the day in 1961 when Alan Shepherd was hurled into space as America's first man in space. I was nowhere near. I was in Kadoka, S.D. A Michigan teen-ager allegedly killed two young sisters and fled. He was arrested in Kadoka, where a nervous sheriff, not used to all the publicity, put him in the jail—a cell in the basement of the court house—until Michigan authorities arrived to take him back to face charges. The sheriff would say nothing, but finally allowed to me that he had had corn flakes for breakfast. With only that detail, Smothers wrote:

> Kennebec, S.D. (UPI)—James Scott Stevens ate cold prison porridge today and awaited a bitter trip homeward for the killing of two young Michigan sisters.

## The Context Paragraph

Put the point of the story, or the contextual paragraph, up high. Did the speaker make the remark in a prepared speech? at a news conference? on the run to a reporter? The Senate passed the tax reform bill. So what: Does it go back to the House? to the president? What is the significance of the bill? We used to call that the "Frandzen graf," so named for Julius Frandzen, the long-time UPI Washington vice president.

## Detail

Look for the telling detail to paint a picture: The winning pitcher sat in front of his locker, peeling an orange as he talked. Add a suprising note: The magnificently fit ballet dancer, Mikhail Baryshnikov, chain-smoked. But the right detail: not "President Ford, twisting his Michigan class ring, signed the mass transit bill today."

Being brief does not mean you sacrifice good detail. Good detail is like a good quote—it adds buoyancy and zest to the story. Being brief requires an acute sense of priority: what's important and what's not.

## Style

The good writer can violate every suggestion I am making. But the beginning writer can't. I recently read John Updike's *Rabbit* trilogy. You may think you can write like Updike and skip all the preparation. You can't. ann kiemel may not capitalize, but you have to. Peter Marshall may have written with all kinds of poetic indentations, but you can't. It's like swimming or dancing. Learn to do it right, and then you can improvise.

# Appendix 2
# Reporting

When asked what are the traits of a good journalist, someone answered: to be nosey and a gossip. There is truth in this: A gossip is insatiably curious, a gossip is the world's best communicator. A good journalist is curious and a communicator.

Don't feel you must refashion your personality—use your strengths to compensate for your weakness. Here are tips:

1. Be curious. Asking questions is to reporting what reading is to writing. Ask questions, ask, ask, ask. Be curious about everything. It is no accident that reporters are best at the game, "Trivial Pursuit."

There are two fundamental questions a journalist can ask in any situation:

—Why?

—What do you mean by that?

2. Develop your own style of asking questions. There are two kinds:

—The rifle shot: "What were you doing last night at ten o'clock?" "Mr. Reagan, when did you first learn of the routing of the proceeds of the Iran arms sales to the contras?"

—The softball (perfected by Bob Scheiffer of CBS and Frank Cormier of the AP): "Mr. Carter, what are you going to do about the energy situation?" This kind of question, carefully used, often puts the source on the defensive because it masks what the reporter might know and requires the source to make a decision on what information to provide.

3. Be ingenious. Be persistent. During Watergate, Woodward and Bernstein sometimes would make a hundred calls to get one small piece of information. One of my chief duties while with UPI in South Dakota was collecting the high school basketball scores. It was unsatisfactory to depend on stringers or students or coaches to call in—they would forget

in the frenzy of a victory or would just plain not do it after a loss. I devised a method of getting the schedules, getting the number of the cafe where everyone gathered after a game—not hard to do in small towns in South Dakota—and then calling that number. The waiter would answer the phone and you could hear the din of the students. I identified myself and asked for the score. She would put down the receiver and shout, "What was the score?" Invariably, someone would shout it out. The whole process often took little more than fifteen to twenty seconds. And never once did I get a complaint that the score was wrong.

4. Know where to go to get information.

—Little information, in the long run, is gained through tips and sleuthing; much more is gained simply by gleaning the public record. A tremendous amount is available through government documents, special interest publications—and the effective reporter often merely pieces all this together. A National Security Agency agent once told me that a high percentage of intelligence is obtained merely by performing this exercise. He said it often is amazing how one insignificant bit of information will complete a massive, complicated puzzle. The Government Press Office in Israel put out a huge amount of information everyday. So do the Government Printing Office and congressional offices in Washington.

—Save articles and clips. This is the most common file for reporters, but one must be wary. An error in a clip (and a news clip is much more likely to have an error than a carefully prepared government document) can lead to the propagation of that error by every reporter using that clip. Thus, the erroneous belief that the Beatles first appeared on the "Ed Sullivan Show," when actually it was on Jack Paar's "Tonight" show. One convenient way to use the clip and avoid any errors is simply to ask your source if he was aware of any errors in the clip.

—Tape important news programs.

—Pay attention to gossip and rumors. I once had a colleague who believed, "If you hear a rumor—it's true." A sixth sense: she could sense when something was up at the White House. Nothing spreads faster than rumors.

5. Go to more than one source. Strive for completeness as well as fairness. One of the biggest problems facing the reporter covering the government is that it's very easy to rely on the official source, who is often very accessible and knowledgeable. Go to the opposition. Go to the special interest group. Check statistics on hunger not only with the government but also with Bread for the World. Most diplomatic reporters fail to use one of the best sources—foreign missions.

6. Keep up to date on what's going on, particularly on your beat. Read the papers, listen to the news. Keep testing your assumptions.

# NOTES

## Chapter 1: *Truth and Untruth*

1. Gerald Priestland, *The Dilemmas of Journalism* (London: Lutterworth, 1979), 113.
2. *The Jerusalem Post Magazine,* 22 March 1985.
3. UPI dispatch, Vienna, 12 Sept. 1985.
4. Priestland, op.cit., 17.
5. Ibid., 36.
6. Sissela Bok, *Lying: Moral Choice in Public and Private Life* (New York: Pantheon, 1978), 25.
7. Ibid., 93.
8. Clifford Christians, "Mass Communications Compromise the Truth," *Media Development* (March 1986):8-11.
9. Ibid., 10-11.
10. See Kenneth L. Pike, "Strange Dimensions of Truth," *Christianity Today* (8 May 1961):692.
11. Jacques Ellul, *The Presence of the Kingdom* (written 1948, New York: Seabury, 1967), 37.
12. Priestland, op.cit., 30.
13. Ibid.
14. Malcolm Muggeridge, *Christ and the Media* (London: Hodder and Stoughton, 1977), 30, 60, 107.
15. Priestland, op.cit., 93.
16. A short survey demonstrates how philosophers define truth. The 17th century's René Descartes wrote that God has given us "a certain faculty of judging" for discerning truth from error, and error results because that power is not infinite (see Descartes' "Of Truth and Error," *Meditations and Selections from the Principles of Philosophy*, trans. John Veitch, LaSalle: Open Court, 1952, 64–65). In the twentieth century, the pragmatist William James wrote: "Truth *happens* to an idea. It *becomes* true, is *made* true by events. Its verity *is* in fact an event, a process" (William James, "Pragmatism's Conception of Truth," *Pragmatism*, written 1907, New York: Longmans, Green, 1949, 201). Bertrand Russell adopted the commonest philosophic view of truth—"that truth consists in some form of correspondence between belief and fact" (Bertrand Russell, "Truth and Falsehood," *Problems of Philosophy*, London: Oxford, 1912, 121). And Sissela Bok wrote that trust in the "principle of veracity," or truthfulness, is foundational to human relationships (Bok, op. cit., 30–31).
17. Peter Gomes, sermon, 15 Feb. 1987.
18. *Seneca's Letters to Lucilius*, XL, trans. E. Phillips Barker, vol. 1 (Oxford: Clarendon, 1932), 124.
19. *New York Herald*, 10 May 1836.

## Chapter 2: *Barriers to Truth*

1. Knowlton Nash, The Inaugural James M. Minifie Memorial Lecture, University of Regina, 5 Oct. 1981.

2. U.S. Senate Watergate hearings, 25 July 1973 (published in *Hearings before the Select Committee on Presidential Campaign Activities of U.S. Senate,* 93rd Congress, Book 6, 2630–31).

3. Justice Hugo Black in majority opinion, *New York Times* v. U.S. and U.S. v. the *Washington Post,* 403 U.S. Reports 717 and 29 Lawyers Edition 2nd, 826.

4. Resolution adopted by First Amendment Congress, Denver, 15 March 1988.

5. Ibid.

6. Sissela Bok, *Secrets: On the Ethics of Concealment and Revelation* (New York: Vintage Books, 1983), 253.

7. See *Freedom at Issue,* no. 100 (January-February 1988), published by Freedom House, 48 East 21st St., New York, N.Y. 10010.

8. Don McNeil, remarks at Institute of Politics, Harvard University, 8 April 1987.

9. *New York Times,* 7 Oct. 1986, A15.

10. *New York Times,* 3 Oct. 1986, A1, A6.

11. Quoted in *Boston Globe,* 6 Oct. 1986, 3.

12. Benjamin C. Bradlee, speech at opening ceremonies of the Joan Shorenstein Barone Center on the Press, Politics and Public Policy, Harvard University, 27 Sept. 1986.

13. Priestland, op.cit., 78.

14. Timothy Crouse, *The Boys on the Bus* (New York: Random House, 1973), 334-35.

15. Priestland, op.cit., 90.

16. Testimony, Senate Watergate hearings, 26 June 1973, op. cit., Book 3, 1094.

## Chapter 3: *Context and Perspective*

1. Priestland, op.cit., 4.

2. Ibid., 18.

3. Ibid., 42.

4. Ibid., 56.

5. *New York Times,* 11 Feb. 1983.

6. Walter H. Brovald, *Good News* (St. Paul, 1980), no. 3.

7. Craig Heaps, *Philosophy of News,* unpublished MS.

8. John Rosselli, quoted in *UPI Reporter,* ed. H.L. Stevenson (New York), 28 Sept. 1972.

## Chapter 4: *Justice, Peace, Morality*

1. Brovald, op.cit., 1982, no. 9.

2. American Society of Newspaper Editors, Washington, D.C., press release, 13 Apr. 1988.

3. *Time's* Distinguished Speakers Program, reported in *Time*, 29 Sept. 1986, 44.

4. Clifford G. Christians, "The Ethical Training of Journalists," *Media Development* 26 (April 1979):20-21.

5. UPI feature, February 1982.

## Chapter 5: *The Power of the Press*

1. Maxwell E. McCombs, *Current Perspectives in Mass Communications Research* (Beverly Hills, Calif.: Sage, 1972), 169.

2. Remarks to Annual Review Meeting, Gannett News Service, Washington, D.C., 13 Dec. 1983.

3. AP dispatch, Porto Alegro, Brazil, 5 July 1980.

4. Priestland, op.cit., 28.

5. Ibid., 29.

6. Michael Gartner, "The First Rough Draft of History," an interview with Benjamin C. Bradlee, *American Heritage* (Oct.-Nov. 1982):37.

7. Bernard Hennessy, *Public Opinion*, 4th ed. (Monterey, Calif.: Brooks/ Cole, 1981), 212.

8. Priestland, op.cit., 107.

9. Hennessy, op.cit., 244.

10. Colin Seymour-Ure, *The Press, Politics and the Public: An Essay on the Role of the National Press in the British Political System* (London: Methuen, 1965), 302.

11. Priestland, op.cit., 106.

12. Seymour-Ure, op.cit., 276.

13. Ibid., 277-78.

14. Richard M. Merelman, *Political Attitudes and Public Opinion*, ed. Dan D. Nimmo and Charles M. Bonjean (New York: David McKay, 1972), 173.

15. Priestland, op.cit., 17.

16. Hennessy, op.cit., 265.

17. Ibid.

18. "The People & the Press," Part 2, *Los Angeles Times Mirror* (1986), 6-7.

19. Spiro T. Agnew, speech at Des Moines, Iowa, 13 Nov. 1969.

20. *'88 Facts about Newspapers* (Reston, Va: American Newspaper Publishers Association), 4.

21. Ibid., 16.

22. Priestland, op.cit., 20.

23. Hennessy, op.cit., 246.

24. Seymour-Ure, op.cit., 301.

25. James R. Beniger, "Media Content as Social Indicators," *Communications Research*, vol. 5 (Beverly Hills, Calif.: Sage), Oct. 1978, 444.

26. Gartner, op.cit., 37-38.

27. Priestland, op.cit., 12-13.

28. Ibid., 13-14.

29. American Newspaper Publishers Association, op.cit., 2.

30. "Nightline," ABC, 10 March 1987.

31. The following material is taken from *Hearings before the Senate Committee on Commerce, Science, and Transportation, on Freedom of Expression*, 28 Sept. 1982, serial no. 97-139, 1-35.

Chapter 6: *Campaigns and Candidates*

1. Panel on "Covering Politics: Responsibilities of Observations and Influence," 20th anniversary of the Institute of Politics, Harvard University, Cambridge, Mass., 9 May 1987 (the same week that the Hart story broke).
2. David S. Broder, remarks at Harvard panel, 9 May 1987.
3. See *Media and Momentum: The New Hampshire Primary and Nomination Politics,* ed. Gary R. Orren and Nelson W. Polsby (Chatham, N.J.: Chatham House, 1987), which produced a map of the United States, pp. 43-44, drawn to the proportion of campaign coverage each state received, making Iowa and New Hampshire loom far larger than California or New York.
4. See *The Great American Video Game: Presidential Politics in the Television Age,* by Martin Schram (New York: William Morrow, 1987).
5. "The Change in Plains," *The Christian Century,* 15 Dec. 1976, 1116-18.
6. "Religionists on the Campaign Trail," *The Christian Century,* 27 Dec. 1972, 1319-20.

Chapter 7: *The White House*

1. See the author's *The Spiritual Journey of Jimmy Carter* (New York: Macmillan, 1978), which arranged and analyzed Carter's religious comments.
2. Remarks to HEW employees, Washington, D.C., 16 Feb. 1977, quoted in *Public Papers of the President, Jimmy Carter, 1977* (Washington, D.C.: Government Printing Office), 167.
3. Address at National Prayer Breakfast, Washington, D.C., 27 Jan. 1977, ibid., 25.
4. Address to the General Council of the World Jewish Congress, Washington, D.C., 2 Nov. 1977, ibid., 1953.
5. Plains, Ga., 8 Jan. 1981, op. cit., 1981. (Washington, D.C.: Government Printing Office), 2869.
6. See the complete results in Linsky's *Impact: How the Press Affects Federal Policymaking* (New York: Norton, 1986).
7. Ibid., Appendix C, 234-42.
8. Interview, *New York Times,* 10 Oct. 1986.
9. See Larry Speakes with Robert Pack, *Speaking Out: The Reagan Presidency from Inside the White House* (New York: Scribners, 1988), 121 and 136.

Chapter 9: *The Foreign Correspondent*

1. Visit to Government Press Office, 2 Apr. 1985.
2. Ze'ev Chafets, *Double Vision: How the Press Distorts America's View of the Middle East* (New York: William Morrow, 1985), 45.
3. Curtis Wilkie, Boston meeting of the American-Arab Anti-Discrimination Committee, 7 Feb. 1987; and David Lamb, the Committee's national convention, Washington, D.C., 4 Apr. 1987.
4. Israel Army Radio newsreel, 25 Feb. 1985.
5. Charles Krauthammer, "Looking Evil Dead in the Eye," *Time,* 15 July 1985, 80.

6. "Does TV Help or Hurt?", *Newsweek*, 1 July 1985, 32.
7. Thomas Griffith, "TV Examines It Excesses," *Time*, 22 July 1985, 61.
8. "King Henry of the Airwaves," *Newsweek*, 1 July 1985, 37.
9. James Kelly, "Caught by the Camera," *Time*, 19 May 1986, 90.
10. "Letting Terrorists Call the Shots", *Newsweek*, 19 May 1986, 66.
11. "Does TV Help or Hurt?", op. cit., 32.
12. Kelly, op. cit.
13. Krauthammer, op. cit.
14. "Letting Terrorists Call the Shots," op. cit.
15. Kelly, op. cit.
16. Krauthammer, op. cit.
17. Jonathan Alter, "Taking Chances," *Newsweek*, 24 March 1986, 60.

## Chapter 10: *Watergate*

1. *King Henry VIII*, act 3, sc. 2, and *Hearings*, op. cit., Book 2, 676.
2. John 3:19, and *Hearings*, ibid., 628.

## Chapter 11: *Briefly, and Finally . . .*

1. *The Christian Century*, 16-23 July 1986, 635.
2. Bruce Manning, quoted in "Response," *UPI Log*, New York, 25 July 1970. Windsor Elliott has now reclaimed her old name of Jenny, and is married to Dr. Os Guinness, a British sociologist who specializes in observing American religion.
3. Cal Thomas, "Not Ready for Prime-Time Prayers," *The Quill*, Oct. 1986, 19.
4. Pete Geiger, Response, *Media Ethics and Responsibility in a Political Context*, Malone College, Canton, Ohio, 9 Feb. 1988.
5. Gary Comstock, unpublished essay.

# Index